UNDERSTAND, IMPROVE

SELF

AND

SOCIETY

UNDERSTAND, IMPROVE
SELF
AND
SOCIETY

SYDNEY L. HERRERA

CITI OF
BOOKS

CITIOFBOOKS, INC.
3736 Eubank NE Suite A1
Albuquerque, NM 87111-3579
www.citiofbooks.com
Hotline: 1 (877) 389-2759
Fax: 1 (505) 930-7244

Ordering Information:

Quantity sales. Special discounts are available on quantity purchases by corporations, associations, and others. For details, contact the publisher at the address above.

Printed in the United States of America.

ISBN-13:   Softcover   979-8-89391-294-4

             eBook   979-8-89391-295-1

Library of Congress Control Number: 2024917800

TABLE OF CONTENTS

PREFACE

Who I am. I am a servant of the Almighty God who has been entrusted with several divine messages, and quite a lot of insight into the nature of who we are, and how we can improve ourselves, our relationships and our societies. I have attempted in this work to deal strictly with issues that affect everyone, without placing everything in the context of what would seem to be a religious work, yet these divine insights are the basis for everything contained in this work.

The three messages with which I have been entrusted are: 1) Our science reveals Gods' methods. 2) The key to meeting God's expectations of us is self-control 3) Diversity is His, as servants we must honor His Diversity.

There are two covenants that I also uphold: I must never denigrate any of His messengers, and I must always respect each individual's divine will. I believe all servants of the Almighty God adhere to these covenants.

As a servant of the Almighty God, I am very much an "anti-cultist". Whereas in cults others are expected to be weaker in the presence of the leader of the cult, so much so that they must follow whatever dogma he or she espouses. I and all who are true servants of the Almighty expect that even though you may come to us, you come to gain strength. You are then expected to go back from whence you came and teach others in your circles with love and understanding for all mankind, so that we build a better world. In this work there is no requirement to follow any dogma. I know that these teachings are meant to strengthen others, as you become stronger you will be more receptive to the teachings of His messengers and His Living Word.

Why this book. This work is focused on the second message and is intended to be of service to all mankind regardless of race, religion, culture or any of the methods that may be devised to separate and divide peoples. It also celebrates both the first and third messages. By providing all with the tools to strengthen themselves and their relationships, they will become more immune to evil, which is dependent on the weaknesses of the will so that it can breach and invade individuals. All can benefit in their day to day activities from having more self-control, stronger wills and seeking to be in balance as they grow rich in life's experiences. As the title suggests, you can read this for understanding only or as a source of material for self- improvement only or you can also apply this information for the benefit of your entire culture and society.

The information here is critical for us to develop, in order to make the transition to a more enlightened civilization, where each world citizen is empowered as an individual. Each would share responsibility to everyone else instead of power being concentrated in the hands of a few who seek to control and often corrupt and destroy the divine will of others.

It is my prayer that you may find some enlightenment in the pages that follow, and that from this day forward you find yourself immensely richer in the true valuables that we can have in this lifetime. The real long- term benefit of this book will be realized if you take the time to perform some of the exercises intended to improving your self-control. The key is closing the gap between thought and action, akin to the difference to your health between learning new exercises and performing those exercises. All talk and good feelings bring only insignificant long-term benefits when compared to focused action. Recognize the value of actions, as actions change outcomes, actions bring results.

SECTION I

PEOPLE

CHILDREN

Surprise package!

Regardless of the circumstances surrounding their birth, all children arrive in this world with the potential to achieve great things for themselves as well as all others. Each child is different from any other who have come before or any who will arrive in the future, and yet, this special life is part of a cycle. Children are eager, willing, and designed to absorb and assimilate from everything and everyone in their environment. Their physical, emotional and spiritual growth is greatly influenced by those with whom they interact and the nature and quality of those interactions. All their senses are tuned to receive, and much like us adults, even those signals that are not processed overtly are received and oftentimes retained.

Their entry into this world represents an extreme contradiction of environments: from a stable, protected and carefully maintained environment, where needs are met automatically, to another, less predictable environment, where but for the care and nurturing of others, their survival would be all but impossible. Yet, this environment allows for development and accomplishments that are impossible in the safety of the womb. Children's primary care-givers, who are also their primary guides and teachers, represent very different types of entities from which the children are to learn and take their cues for all that is to come during their lives. An adaptation of the old adage that says "Show me yo@ur friends and I'll tell you about who you are" is never more apt than when applied to children as in "Show me some children and I'll tell you much about their parents".

Guide and teacher?

All who come in contact with the young can be teachers. Parents have an obligation to be both teachers and guides. Except for a life of devotion to the common good of all mankind, there is no more significant task than being effective guides and teachers to our offspring. By being effective teachers, parents make their work as guides easier. If however they do not spend the time and effort necessary to be efficient and effective teachers, they make their foremost functions as guides very difficult, if not impossible.

When we are blessed with children, it is as if we are given charge of a group of explorers to lead on a guided tour. The number of our charges that we successfully lead through the hazards, distractions and even perils of the journey, is a measure of ourselves, especially our faithfulness to our duty as parents as well as our own usefulness and effectiveness.

It should be the goal of every guide to deliver everyone entrusted to his or her care safely, and with a wealth of knowledge and good experiences at the appointed destination at the end of their guided tour. All involved in the upbringing of children should be measured by the results of their work as observed in the well-being of the children they raise, as well as the levels of development reached by each child in relation to their ability to productively reside with, and positively co-exist with others in their environment.

Our charges should be educated in our customs and values, they should be knowledgeable and well rounded to demonstrate how effective we have been as guides and teachers. There should be no acceptable excuses for not successfully delivering every child placed in our care at the end of our stewardship.

The quality of the child that is developed in their care is a measure of every parent. There is no greater responsibility than preparing a child to the maximum of their abilities, with knowledge of their culture, and responsibility and respect to assume their place in this world. As with all things, our values in regards to our society, as well as the resulting rewards, should be measured by the quality of the product and services we provide to that society. This is especially crucial when the product is our eventual replacements as they represent the future of the culture and values of the society. Thus, we as guides should face sincere scrutiny based on the quality of our work!

One of the most important skills that we must strive to master is the art of redirection. The young are very impressionable and if we are able to master this vital skill, we will find that keeping our charges content and working in the direction that we would like them to, is not very difficult, but it does indeed entail quite a bit of subtle redirecting their focus, and thus their energies, to the tasks with which we would like them to be involved.

Redirection is a skill that as responsible adults, we all have and practice everyday: we use redirection skills to ensure that we prioritize tasks, and keep our focus tuned to any chosen task. Redirection is what we use when we perform one task while excluding other activities which we then identify as background noise. However, achieving conscious mastery of redirection is what gives us the ability to be subtle and enjoy the harmony we all seek, while using our ability to refocus any child's efforts to where we intend.

As with all skills, we should focus on being positive, even when we are teaching consequences. Let's look at the following example: a young child is focused on obtaining a certain item and becomes upset because he or she cannot have that item. If we are adept at redirecting, we can refocus their attention based on color, size or some other attribute, or to another similar item or, simply redirect their attention to another activity. Older children can be taught to redirect simply based on non-verbal clues that we teach them to associate with certain behaviors, this is a skill that has been in all our families seemingly forever, remember how our involved parents or grandparents used subtle ways to have us perform as they wished? We as parents and guides need to relearn this skill, so that these valuable pieces of our cultures can be passed down to our offspring for their benefit.

We are their guides, and thus, we are responsible for keeping them educated to any dangers along their journey, and we must be ready to intervene, if necessary, to ensure none are lost to the quicksand, waterfalls and ravenous animals which are just off the path we should know as guides. All those who have gone ahead of us have taken the time to lead us on that path, so we must know it! It is a travesty to throw up our hands and say "I do not know what to do" when it comes to guiding or educating our children, because we have had so many who taught and guided us!

It is also our responsibility to ensure the education of our charges, so that they are not swayed by the smooth talkers who line all the paths, and are experts at misleading and stealing our charges. If we do not place enough weight to this responsibility, we risk our charges not being at the assigned delivery location where they branch off and assume responsibility for their own their journeys – with all requisite skill for success.

The paths of many other individuals will at different times intersect with us and our charges, and many of them will have our children best interests at heart, but, we must realize that paths that intersect do not serve the same purpose as our paths, which is the one that should lead our charges to their destination. We must always be consistently working to deliver all our charges to the prearranged dropping off point of adulthood - enriched by our culture and with the knowledge and skills to pursue their own journeys.

As will be explained in a later section "Improving, Adapting", we should always employ the 'village principle' and whenever possible choose experienced relationship mentors. We must be especially wary of those who seek to direct us, but whose journeys do not contain examples of them providing guidance to their own children. How can anyone be of assistance to us in our duties if they shirk their own duties? How can they help you guide our children, if they are unwilling or unable to guide their own? This is notwithstanding any social, political or educational achievements that they may have accomplished. Just because someone is adept at financial matters does not mean they are good with people in general, and specifically, they may be a total failure in raising their own children!

Recognize that our life journeys will be filled with positive experiences when we learn from the experiences of others we admire, and disregard those who have no relevant experience, but are willing to experiment with our works and our precious cargo! How effective a teacher can we really be if we cannot teach those dearest to us? A quick head count and quality check on those put into our care at the drop off point will show the quality of our being. Are you doing the work necessary to deliver all your charges at the drop off point? Are you satisfied that they are being groomed to be future teachers and guides, or future leaders?

Since there is no more important duty than to deliver all our charges from birth to adulthood with the best preparation available to continue their journeys, we must focus our energies on being effective teachers and prepared guides when we seek to become or are placed in the role of parents and mentors.

Where does this road lead?

Children will always want to wander at some point, either to "discover" new things, or because they are enticed to follow something that piques their interest. We must be sufficiently engaged with our children, so that we are aware of when this is occurring. A well equipped guide will be prepared to provide education and support, either by being available, or finding and making resources available to both teach, and assist as children gain their own experiences in "finding out where that road leads".

Whenever we come to a part of the journey where our charges want to venture into an area of which we have little or no knowledge, we can yet be examples of resourcefulness. We as parents can achieve this by both our demeanor and aptitude in finding other resources to provide either preparatory or support information, both prior to and while our charges explore any area of interest with which we may not be familiar. For example, if one of our charges is pursuing a field of study or activity with which we are unfamiliar, we can be examples of how to find support groups or information, and be involved until we recognize that the individual needing the information is once again comfortable. Much of this recognition of comfort is the result of being observant over time with each of our charges.

The critical significance of ages three to eleven (The "3211")

Although each child is different and very few generalizations on character fit all children, the years three through eleven are almost uniformly critical in cementing of the values that persist throughout their entire lives.

The 3211 is that period when the culture and those values that are to be passed down from the parents must be taught and demonstrated repeatedly, along with all acceptable societal values, so that as a young adult is formed soon afterwards, all that is required is gentle reinforcement of what is already learned. If these years are not utilized in this manner, it will be very difficult, well nigh impossible to direct these young adults to these values.

The 3211 is also the period when children like sponges, soak up whatever are the dominant influences around them. If parents neglect to be the source of the culture and values, this neglect will not preclude children from being sponges. Unfortunately, what happens however, is that they soak up and retain the values of others instead of their parents. Parents who ignore, or do not place adequate importance on their duties in transferring their culture and values during this critical period, will in time come to learn that their children have absorbed behaviors and values that may not be based in the culture of the parents. Depending on the degree of negligence, children may not only fail to learn the culture and values of their parents, but even worse, based on the sources from which they absorb culture and values, they may indeed learn to ignore their parents' values. As a consequence, when they become teenagers and young adults, they may to choose to completely reject any attempts by these formerly negligent parents to impart values or customs. This is the juncture where most parents who end up with 'difficult' children create and foster the issues that become apparent in 'problem' teenagers!

Many parents who raise children while themselves rebelling against the culture and values of their parents will find that they are in fact teaching rebellion from parental cultures and values to their young children by their words and actions. Culture and values cannot be replaced by a void, as by the time the child becomes a teenager, every child has a set of values that he or she has learnt during the 3211. Whether these "values" are a product of the diligent work of their parents or guardians however is the only thing that may be in question.

One can not learn culture and values solely through the acquisition of physical objects. Many parents who are negligent in their duties of transferring culture to their children may chooseto provide money or anything that money can buy instead of spending time with their children and teaching them many things. These teachings can range from what to eat and how to prepare their food, to sharing anecdotes from their family histories, while teaching and demonstrating the values that are admirable in their culture. Remember, during these formative years, children soak up information like sponges, if you are not a major factor in their learning, it does not mean that they will not learn. What it means is that they will not learn from you!

If you let the values portrayed in the media, such as television, or demonstrated by others around you, appear to be acceptable to you, or you fail to perform those actions to provide alternatives, your children learn that these behaviors are acceptable. As a consequence, they will soon enough enact some of these same behaviors! It is very important that when your children observe actions that are not acceptable to you, that you reinforce in them that these actions are not to be emulated. It is important to recognize that our charges learn more from observing our behaviors than by simply listening to what we say to them. Thus, _consistent actions over time_ is required, so that children learn to emulate those aspects of ourselves that we would admire in others.

As part of their childhood emotional development, all children want our acceptance and adulation, and we should provide this as much as possible. However, there will be times when we must inform our children that certain behaviors are unacceptable, and that there can be negative consequences to certain actions. If we are adept at nurturing, providing support and encouragement, our children will quickly learn to avoid those actions and behaviors that evoke negative emotions and unpleasant consequences. Thus, they get better at making choices that lead to positive outcomes. It is not very difficult to establish those boundaries outside which our children know their actions are not acceptable or are not permitted. What is required is consistency on our part, along with love and support when they stay within those lines. Eventually, given the predictable options, they will be the children that we love and admire, and we become better guides and teachers.

One of the reasons we may overlook unbecoming behavior in our children is that we always want them to be happy. But if we choose to ignore actions that we know will lead to negative consequences in the future for the benefit of avoiding discomfort or conflict in the present, we are simply responding blindly to our emotions. Emotions have no vision, they are about now. This is why we need to seek balance so that even though we enjoy our emotional interactions with our children, we won't loose sight of where these actions may lead. Examples can be found in eating and study habits. If we introduce vegetables to children when they are very young, they grow up just knowing it as something to eat,. However, if we are not persistent at first (and we may have to practice some redirection – "in comes the plane!" as we pretend they are a landing strip for the vegetables!) even though we know it is for their future benefit, they learn very quickly that their resistance results in them having it their way. The result for the present may seem to be the harmony we desire, but the future is now clouded…. This principle also applies to children completing homework assignments, or exhibiting rude or disrespectful behavior.

The key is for us to gain the inner strength to have the balance to hold our emotions in check and insist that our children perform to the values that we teach and demonstrate along with appropriate rewards for their accomplishments. Even if they are not endowed with special abilities, as we provide the support necessary while overcoming any short term negative emotional events, our vision is allowing us to endow their future with many positive attributes, such as honesty, tenacity, respect, tolerance etc.

After this period of purely following their guides and soaking up everything like a sponge, children are apt to start exploring, even challenging some of those values and customs we may have imparted to them, however once a thing is learned it is not unlearned, and so the early teaching and guidance is entrenched in their character and stays there even if awareness of these values and customs do not ensure their conformity.

The bonding that is formed during the 3211 endures, it is what makes sibling bonds last a lifetime. It is therefore critical that the needs of the young be met by those who will be forming bonds and will be part of their circle of trust. Many parents make the mistake of abandoning the opportunities of enrichment which are presented once during this special period in a child's life, by absconding or allowing others to make use of this opportunity. As a consequence, the parents will then have to attempt to teach their values and principles to their children in their teenage years! These are the parents who "loose touch" with their children when they become teenagers, because at that time, these children are not accustomed to looking to these parents for clues as to how to behave, and the teenagers may find all these "new" rules that the parents are now trying to impose unwelcome.

Even though children can grow up and choose their own paths to follow, this crucial point bears repeating: the bedrock of their characters is set during the 3211. The principles and disciplines which are taught during this critical period determines how much of the parents culture is passed down to the next generation. Thus, parents must pay special attention to ensuring that these formative years are not left as teaching opportunities at the discretion to others. This is especially important if parents are concerned about having continuity in their family trees, and want the values and culture which were handed down to them by previous generations to be passed on to the next generation. Paying attention and being in control of teaching opportunities is a must and care must be taken that these opportunities are not left to substiture caregivers such as nannies (except in cases of trusted family members or others of the same culture) or to pseudo- caregivers like the electronic media (TV/Internet etc.).

FEMALES

Nature and nurture

Culture is the bedrock of a society. Women are the foundations of any society. Any society is strongest when it's women are educated in and committed to the continuation of their culture. Strong and virtuous women are assets to any culture or society, they are in fact some of its most valuable assets. Women without virtues however, can be a severe liability, so much so that they may bring discredit to the entire society.

Women are given the task and the critically important duty of installing the values and much of the culture that must be passed down in any society. Although we all can foster these abilities, through their instinctive nurturing skills, women are prepared to implement this process during the mentoring they provide during the critical years of any offspring. Through the female gifts of nurturing, protecting and caring for the young, they become examples of what is best in all of us. The value of this responsibility may not be recognized in monetary terms in modern societies, which unfortunately is an indictment of the weaknesses inherent in the design of modern society. Yet this lack of societal recognition does not negate the significance of the crucial role women play. All acceptable behaviors, customs, and foods in most societies which focus on the continuation of their cultures, are passed down, mainly through the care and nurturing of women.

In order to be successful in this extremely important role, to be the true foundation of a society however, women must be anchored to the bedrock, which is the culture of their predecessors. Because without special effort, many women are prone to responding to their emotional needs more than their physical or spiritual needs, as a result, without a basis in culture, these women may forfeit long- term benefits for short-term harmony, as is the wont of the emotions. Thus, culture serves to constantly remind them of their special place and responsibilities.

Any individual can consciously attain a balance which enables them to achieve their personal goals,. Females who primarily seek appeasement of their emotional needs however are likely to engage in behaviors that may lead to the short term realization of acceptance and adulation, but can result in discarding values and principles, which in turn compromises the cornerstones of their parent culture. Repetition of this pattern by many females can lead to wholesale changes across the entire culture or society, from the lack of key values, like respect and discipline being passed down to the next generation, to being exploited and fostering an entire generation of individuals who are susceptible to being exploited by those who consciously or otherwise recognize their susceptibility to their emotional needs.

When a matriarchal figure such as a grandmother, mother or other female member is a balanced leader in a household, all who spend time in her presence will benefit and be enriched by the culture and values she teaches, for even discipline is given as a part of a nurturing relationship. All behaviors can be influenced by the actions of a strong, balanced and well grounded female.

However, if the women in a household, society or culture reject those values and customs, which have distinguished and have governed the acceptable behaviors of that culture, unfortunately, within two generations, all that has been passed down from countless previous generations before can be lost.

All cultures have unwritten rules for the passing of cultural torches from mothers to daughters, which run the full gamut of human behaviors. These unwritten rules then get passed down with some modifications to the next generation. However, as should be apparent this is somewhat of a delicate chain, which can be broken very readily by the will of either generation of females, or even others who gain the confidence of either mother or daughter.

Many females are dominated by their emotional needs, thus they may expend a lot of effort in activities that are geared towards receiving acceptance and adulation. Unfortunately, the emotions are not tied to vision, and as such are not concerned with anything but the present. Thus, those who place their emotional needs above all others are likely to cast aside long- held customs, which may be for the long -term benefit of the culture or society, for the satisfaction of their immediate emotional needs. In the extreme, all long- term benefits to the culture or society are likely to be compromised by these individuals.

It is for these reasons that, unknowingly, in many male dominated cultures, women are treated as second class citizens. Inherent in the behaviors displayed in those societies are the recognition of the importance to be attached to a virtuous woman, as well as the scorn and ostracizing of women without the recognized cultural virtues. In these societies the following extreme contrasting behaviors can be observed: women are so revered that no one is allowed to disrespect the mother or sister of anyone without reprisal, however women who are even suspected of not upholding the values of the culture may receive the worst reprisals available in the society. These behaviors are based on the unconscious and instinctive recognition that women are the true foundations of the society. It is this desire to protect what is important that leads to the oppressive rules by those who may not fully understand the reasons behind their own behaviors. This book is not meant to condone these behaviors, but rather to explain it, in an effort to make all involved and the concerned can understand this phenomenon, with the hope that they will then find the means to work towards the benefit of all involved. In a transformed world, all females would not only be treasured, but they would be educated on their special status and responsibility, as well as their abilities to surmount any obstacles. Thus, the entire society benefits from stronger, enlightened, dedicated and virtuous foundations firmly implanted in the bedrock.

As in most things, results are what matters -except of course, in bureaucracy, where the only things that matters are processes! In order to improve anything, we must first seek to understand that which we seek to improve. In the process we are improved by our diligence, patience and ability to place aside preconceptions to allow ourselves to grow in knowledge.

Everyone is a product of their emotional, physical, and spiritual components. Through practice all individuals can develop these components to achieve some balance within themselves. Learning is accomplished both consciously as well as unconsciously (the subconscious), the enlightened among us are those who have an awareness of, as well as learn from, certain experiences which most people may encounter only through their subconscious. Women are often blessed with these abilities which are often referred to as intuition and through this they can improve themselves and their lot by becoming more aware of the invaluable and unique roles that they play in all societies. Woman can then become the models of society that even the powerful recognize. These leaders in turn will come to realize that the preeminence of strong, balanced women does not mean that the continuation of their cultures are threatened by any lack of cultural values and virtues.

It is important that words which indicate balance and strength be verified by consistent actions. Individuals who establish a pattern that demonstrates a lack of self-control over both the physical and emotional needs are prone to be denied the trust of others who can discern that these individuals are either unwilling or incapable of backing up their words with actions. Others seek to profit from these weaknesses, which has resulted in the proliferation of many "feel good now" schemes, these are represented by the many schemes often connected to managing weight as well as the abundance of advertising geared to give an immediate sense of wellbeing based on purchases of goods and services.

The weak will not take the time to realize that happiness, contentment, and even true acceptance and adulation are based on their inner strengths and character, which by developing their component strengths can be attained in form of balance and control over the responses to their emotional, physical and spiritual needs.

In every culture there are stories of great women, who have developed their spiritual and physical components and taken control of their emotional needs, so that they are not swayed by the "feel good now" pressures, but have dedicated themselves to achievements that benefit entire societies. They serve as examples of what is possible with dedication and a commitment to a chosen cause. What is different about these females is that they have learnt to develop their inner strength, in order to go against the conventional wisdom. This takes both physical strength, and more importantly spiritual strength to be able to persevere, and endure the almost inevitable hardships that go with "swimming against the tide" in any society. Emotions are good for the beginning and end of the journey, the physical and spiritual are what provide the fuel and endurance for the duration.

We are not all born leaders and there are additional burdens heaped on leaders that would bend or even break the multitudes they lead. These leaders, however, are the individuals who take the risks and make those decisions which light the path for all who follow. It is indeed a travesty that any society should institute a prejudicial system which denies the full participation and contribution of whole classes based on a criteria such as gender, without giving gifted individuals of that gender the opportunity to serve. As a result of this injustice is that these societies never achieve real balance or their full potential because many true leaders that are born within these societies are suppressed. Many females, though not unaccustomed to sacrifice, must develop vision and the ability to deal with power dispassionately, as true leaders are either born with these abilities or must develop them. Societies need to recognize and accept the contributions of these leaders who, when they are female, may provide solutions by bringing a fresh and unique perspective to many issues.

Alas, not all are leaders, and as such many women dominated by their emotional needs project an image of being only concerned with seeking adulation and doing things that feel good now, as such they may appear as though they cannot be trusted to make tough decisions today to affect a better tomorrow for the next generation. Can this be changed? Absolutely! Just as we can lose the heritage that should be passed down within two generations, within two generations all women can learn to develop the awareness of their component needs and the techniques to achieve harmony through balance and control over their innate emotional, physical and spiritual needs. These enlightened women would never evoke fears of cultural debasement from others due to weaknesses. They are not devoid of emotions and emotional needs, as these attributes may in fact be heightened, which may bring added benefits for all they embrace into their circles. Through vision, self-control and spiritual awareness, these females will develop a balance that allows them to embody the very best of their culture, regardless of the role they assume in the society. In time, there will be no need to debate their abilities based on the choices that they make, because all will know that their decision making is sound and not just based on quirks of emotions.

Using the power of words, any enlightened individual can appear to place a woman's emotional needs as a priority of their actions, and thus many females who respond primarily to their emotional needs can be unwittingly influenced. As an example, a male who appears to place a female's happiness today as one of his priorities can easily befriend any woman who is dominated by her emotional need. This also applies to her being convinced that by purchasing some item, she will attain more acceptance and adulation. This item will become a priority to her, thus the trends in advertising! So the appeasement of the current emotion is a vulnerability that may in fact become a liability as can be evidenced by females who may befriend unsavory characters who fulfill their emotional needs, or by overextending their purchasing ability, or indulging in other compromising behaviors, which could have negative effects on all around them in the future. But these are the ways of the emotions, because unfortunately emotions are not unduly encumbered by the weight of vision.

For most females a somewhat difficult balance has to be attained, when controlling the emotions as emotions are a significant part of being female, and it is one of the defining characteristics that lead to the quest for "beauty and harmony now", which is also a part of instinctive nurturing, which is natural to every female. The objective should not be to suppress the emotions, but rather to develop the physical and spiritual components, so that the significance of these component rise, and they serve to provide a balance in the responses to the needs of the emotional component. Females who seek to suppress their emotional component risk being perceived as not being female and some of the best female experiences may not be attainable.

That health and relationships are two of their most valuable possessions should be taught early on and priority should be placed upon passing on a desire to continually increase the wherewithal required to successfully attain and have very high quality of both health and relationships. The relationship between good food, good health, feeling and looking good, as well as caring for oneself and those they nurture, should be constantly emphasized.

Strengths and weaknesses

The primary and greatest strengths of females are based on, and geared towards, their gifts of nurturing. When exerted with concerted effort, they can change the direction of a society through their commitment and fortitude. Care must be taken, however, to ensure that not too much energy is expended" looking back", and that more is committed to being forward looking, and performing the visionary work today to ensure the smooth progression into the journey ahead.

Control of the emotions allow for the development of vision by affording the enjoyment of experiences, which are a result of planning, and the satisfaction gained from the successful execution of long- term plans. These positive experiences are the basis for both, teaching and reinforcing the benefits of being able to control the short-term urges of emotions for the discipline and sacrifices that result in planning for the future.

A foundation anchored in bedrock is not easily destroyed, so too are females nurtured in a culture based on strong values. Many individuals who seek to dislodge females from this foundation may or may not be aware of the damage they do to the individual, culture and society. A foundation not attached to bedrock is no longer worth being called a foundation, and women without the basis of culture are more likely to indulge in behaviors that are the result of emotional needs regardless of the long- term repercussions. Therefore, it is vitally important that awareness of culture be taught to all females, especially the young. This early teaching of culture enables those who move between cultures to place priority on learning the nuances of their adopted culture, where hopefully there are no severe conflicts with their previous culture. These females will also be properly equipped, to make a sound choice of how and what they assimilate in situations where there are conflicts that cause stressful discomfort.

For families, we must recognize just as with critical genetic materials, females are the conduits for the continuation of the family lines. It is especially important to educate all young females of the powers they have as keepers of our cultures and heritage as passed down through the generations. It would be advisable to use "the 3211" to instill the values and all other aspects of culture that empower them to make the wise choices, which bring honor to the family, and to avoid those situations and decisions that cause unfortunate consequences for all. The key is the empowerment of these females, and this effort should be undertaken by all members who have a vested interest in their development.

Ideally, assuming values of another culture would not be seen as a weakness, but as added strength as a solid base of values and recognition of their roles and responsibilities to the continuation of the culture and heritage of their ancestors has been established and all can trust that they will be honored.

Males

Nature and nurture

Males are by nature, subjects normally dominated by their physical component. Since the ultimate achievement of the physical is power, this pre-occupation with things physical result in most males being susceptible to taking any action that lead to them being viewed as being powerful.

In order to obtain, as well as to maintain, this objective of power, there is some measure of control of the emotions, or detachment from emotional needs as well as the practice of even basic visionary disciplines. This is because oftentimes there is some amount of planning and execution to obtain and/or retain power.

The most valuable asset any man can have is his vision. When coupled with perseverance and dedication, visionaries can, and often will, move entire civilizations. Men without vision, however, are more prone to be reactive and, although they may be effective, the results of their actions will most likely be only incidental in the future. Real visionaries however affect the future in ways that are more pronounced than many who observe their actions can foresee.

Each of us has an independent will, we can choose to develop ourselves and strengthen our wills so that we can take control of our basic and instinctive urges. This self-control is what facilitates the discipline required to excel in anything we choose. We all have some measure of self-control, conscious development however affords us the discipline to grow and develop those traits that we admire or deem necessary to be successful in achieving whatever goals we may set for ourselves. Since most men are normally dominated by their physical component, normally, their most desired objective and highest accomplishment is power. However, without the development of self-control, this power will often be misused. We are not, however, such simple creatures that only one of our needs is evident in our beings, and we are not incapable of mastery of our urges, egos and emotions. This ability for improvement is the main reason for this work – that we, through understanding, learn to improve ourselves, and hopefully we'll be able to improve, all with whom we come in contact, by educating them as well. As a result, we can improve our societies and eventually this entire world.

All the young should be encouraged to first understand and then build the ability for self-control. They should be taught the concept of balancing their responses to the needs and the control of their emotional, physical and spiritual components. Due to young males' preoccupation with power, they should especially be aided in recognizing their ability to control and develop balance in order to achieve their fullest potential. While they learn through play, they should be taught that developing the ability to always practice taking the "big" view of activities around them,. They also should be taught to take control of their emotions, so that their actions are geared to be of maximum effect in this "big" picture. The ability for emotional control will assist them in performing at higher levels as well as recognizing their potential to achieve any goals that they may set for themselves.

Because of the propensity to be dominated by their physical needs, and the possibility for detrimental acts based on overdependence of projecting their power through physical means, it is important that young males be made aware of actions and consequences early in their lives, so that vision can be fostered as a part of their education. Being dominated by the physical makes one more likely to respond to the physical, so efforts to use emotionally based stimulus may only result in frustration and misunderstanding by all parties involved. Thus, it is important for the guide to develop some knowledge of the component that dominates any child, in order to effectively teach, control or redirect that individual. This is restating the simple rule of "understand in order to be effective". It is a significant part of the reason boys need interaction and direction from other males (dads!), not only do they have others to emulate, but they also have others who have shared experiences and experienced similar component needs, and thus can relate to them very effectively based on real empathy and at a non-verbal level because of this common bond. There is also less denial of who they may be ("it is what it is!") based on a shared understanding of the causes of non –verbal component needs, as well as effective alternate ways to meet or redirect these non- verbal component needs.

Intrinsic abilities should be nurtured in all, but teachings should be geared to heighten an awareness of what is common to all, as well as ensuring that young males are steeped in both history and culture. This will serve to provide them with a basis for a vision of the future. Regardless of whether they are dealing with others in their personal lives, family circles or at large within the society, their actions will have a foundation in the knowledge of the past, and their actions are thus more likely to influenced by the present circumstances as well as their vision of the future.

Along with being taught vision and self-control, young men should be made aware of an expectation of reliability and purpose from their early years. They must be informed that they should strive to be measured not only by personal accomplishments, which demonstrate their talents, but also by what they leave in their wake, especially in regards to who and how many people benefit from their efforts. If they are successfully taught these values, they will grow up to be better individuals because they understand that others depend on them to be effective in whatever tasks they are assigned, and their actions are interrelated to the success of more than just themselves.

One very important rule which must be taught and passed down as an asset to all young men is the "valuation of values". This is very important, not only to reinforce the values that they should seek to engender and project themselves, but also so they learn to treasure those who embody values that they admire. This will eventually lead them to place more weight to the character of those they encounter and less on the flashy displays that some individuals are wont to enact or purely physical appearances.

If we are effective in teaching this "valuation of values", the effects will be visible in the friends that these young men keep, as well as the place of prominence that they assign to them. This principle also will affect the next generation by their eventual choice of a partner based on the values that they seek. Often this choice will subconsciously be based on the very best of the females they have had contact with during their formative years. Young men should also be made aware of the fact that, even though we may all seem to be different, and we may seek different goals, we may still, however, share some of the same underlying values and that the real differences between peoples are most related to their different cultural backgrounds. It is also important to teach that we become stronger when we are able to strengthen those around us and we are at our best when we make use of the strengths of our partners.

Strengths and weaknesses

Considering the fact that males are somewhat more responsive to their physical component and the ultimate need for power and control, it is important that males be taught to recognize that there are some very important attributes that are not dependent solely on physical ability. The roles that are played by all the women they encounter from their youth and as they go through their adult lives are of significant importance. They should be made aware of the difference in the effect of their actions on the emotions of females, as compared to other males.

It will be beneficial to the entire society, and young males in particular, if they are taught how deeply the behaviors of most females are tied to their emotional needs. Along with the awareness necessary to discern dominant component needs, young men should also be taught that the level of success they have in dealing with females depends largely on the degree of awareness they have in recognizing the significance of that individual's emotional needs.

This awareness and resulting abilities should be actively cultivated from the time young males are able to discern the result of their actions. One of the benefits of this type of awareness is that these young males will soon recognize that females possess abilities that are not only complementary, but may far exceed their own. When this awareness is raised, we are more likely to have these young men willing to work in harmony with all others based on their abilities instead of any preconceived notions of what these abilities may be, or any assumed shortcomings based on gender, race, ethnicity or culture.

That fact that health and relationships are two of their most valuable possessions should be taught early on, and priority should be placed upon passing on a desire to continually increase the wherewithal required to successfully attain and have very high quality of both. That food makes us stronger and enables us to stay healthier should be constantly emphasized. The quality and diversity of food and food's effects on health should be stressed in an effort to encourage a willingness to at least sample all natural foods, based on the assumption that there may be benefits that are not yet described by our current scientific literature. If a correlation between healthy eating habits and their physical state is established early in their lives, young males can be guided to healthy eating with little effort, due to their susceptibility to their physical component need and desire to be strong and powerful.

SECTION II

RELATIONSHIPS

ONE OF OUR MOST VALUABLE POSSESSIONS!

From the time we enter until the time we exit this phase of existence, relationships are one of the two most valuable things that we can acquire. However, sometimes in the middle of our journeys we may become a little confused by the noise created by many around us, possibly even to the extent that we may come to believe that other achievements or objectives may be more valuable. Yet, nothing could be further from the truth.

This point is worth repeating: the two most valuable possessions anyone can have are good health and good relationships!

From birth through death (transformation) other objects and achievements may be very useful in enhancing both health and relationships. But without health or relationships the attainment of personal goals will not only be empty but also not truly gratifying. Imagine for a minute that you were indeed the richest person on the planet, but you had a terrible ailment or your riches could not be comfortably shared with anyone. Yes, you would be able to attract almost anyone to share your possessions, but what if none of these people really cared about you, if none wanted to spend time with you alone just to enjoy your company, or had any interest in your other personal aspirations? In short, everyone you encountered was focused on getting something from you! How depressing would it be to realize that you are functionally alone and would continue to be that way regardless of the size of the crowd you attracted?

Relationships are like offspring and all relationships are personal, although the context of the relationship may vary. They are created through communication, and just like children, at first they need to be carefully nourished and nurtured. Indeed, relationships always need some attention if they are to flourish. As with our offspring, relationships develop based on the ingredients used to nourish them, and therefore good relationships should not be contaminated with greed, jealousy or distrust if we would like to maintain these relationships.

We must learn to review the state of all our relationships, being aware, that the health and wellbeing of each relationship is dependent on all the parties involved. There can be seriously dysfunctional relationships based on uneven participation or even flawed and/or unrealistic expectations. Like us, relationships exist in the present, but they are also a product of the past of each individual involved. It is very important to note that we cannot make relationships better by projecting our aspirations or wishes for the future into them, as they are immune from that type of manipulation. This projection may only serve to introduce undue stresses into the relationship based on possibly selfish expectations which are not communicated to other parties in the relationship!

The more we know about ourselves, the more self-control that we have, the more likely we can sincerely present ourselves as pleasant parties with whom others can delight in sharing a relationship.

One of the keys to having positive relationships is through self-control, ***consciously seeking to focus on what we have in common with others in the relationship,*** this is extremely important! In order to attain mastery in this critical area of human interactions, we must attain a level of self-control that enables us to be observant and attentive to other individuals' demands and aspirations. We must learn to glean from both, verbal and non-verbal communications, what component needs are dominant in these individuals and from these observations and any shared interests we will then be able to present that side of ourselves which is interesting and maybe even pleasant to any individual.

Does that mean that we should seek to be agreeable to everyone with whom we seek to have a good relationship? No, and by all means we may have sincere disagreements with people we care about, it is more important that we be knowledgeable and thus interesting. It is then that we may be able to bring a new viewpoint and be of value to others.

Sydney stopped here!

These principles are on display in every relationship as the following examples demonstrate, please feel free to add your own. Sports fans may support different teams but the shared interest in the sport can serve to create relationships. With self-control and awareness, one would focus on the technical aspects of the sport, i.e. demonstrate your knowledge, as in a discussion of what makes a good goalie/quarterback/pitcher/bowler etc., and be willing to concede that their opinion of the best player at a certain position has certain shortcomings when measured against another player, who in turn would also have their own shortcomings. In another context, employees are screened via the employment process to ensure that they have a certain set of skills, if nothing else, this screening would be the basis of a shared set of interests.

Here's another example: whether it is progressing in the chosen field, or deciding on what is done with the proceeds of their employment, business partners (including romantically linked couples) have a shared interest in working together to attain certain financial goals, and there may be other shared interest in how these finances are invested or disposed off.

Since culture is like a river in which we are all immersed, we may have shared aspirations with almost everyone we meet based on our common cultural upbringing. This may be in addition to any of the many other facets of our current existence, and focusing on these shared interests is the basis for good relationships. We all have many short- term relationships with people who serve us or who we serve, from waiters/waitresses, and taxi drivers to secretaries and our elected officials. If we show some interest in them and at least try to be pleasant for the duration of any interaction, by exercising self-control for that period of time, we are more likely to gain a positive reaction and an overall pleasant experience. We cannot control others, and if we learn the exercises given in the section "Improving, Adapting" we will be able to walk away without too much negative baggage, even when we encounter individuals who do not respond positively to our demeanor, or have to interact with individuals whose actions may be viewed as not in our best interests, during the period in which we needed their services.

With all relationships, we must understand the principle of personal circles. Except for family members, those close to us would be individuals we actively choose to be in our inner circles. Through exercising our knowledge and self-control, we need to be aware of and respond to their component needs over extended periods. We also need to be able to attain some level of harmony with those we encounter who may exist outside our close, inner personal circles. We need to increase our awareness so that we are able to 'read', and appropriately respond very quickly to individuals outside our personal circles so we can pleasantly achieve our objectives before moving on with our lives. We must be very conscious of creating and maintaining personal circles. We need to be observant and use our senses proportionately (two eyes, two ears, one mouth!), so that we observe and listen twice as much as we speak so that we can determine whether the individuals we encounter are people that we would bring into our homes and share our deepest secrets or are persons with whom we spend time only when sharing a common interest (party, sports, work etc.). We also need to always evaluate how our values are complimentary to theirs and where there are serious contradictions. This will enable us to very quickly determine how closely we embrace and consciously decide into which of our personal circles we would want to place this individual.

With self-control we can learn to smile, to present ourselves always as positive and ready to make someone else smile, even when the role that we are playing demands that we perform some function that may not always be pleasant. By using our self-control we can consciously separate our roles from our character. Not realizing this important concept is a common shortcoming of many of the unenlightened, who see their assigned role as the basis for their personal character. If we are to improve ourselves, we must have a very distinct sense of our identity, which must be independent of any role someone may assign to us as part of employment or otherwise.

We must realize that in all our relationships we must first seek to understand that which we seek to change, whether it be within ourselves, or whether we intend to influence a change in someone with whom we interact. If we do not take the time to understand, we risk the somewhat comical cycle of repeating the same action, but expecting different results, which is often referred to in jest, as the classical definition of madness.

At this juncture, it is pertinent that we acknowledge one very important point: in order to experience and develop great relationships we must have an understanding of ourselves. We must have completed an examination of ourselves, so that we know what are our core values. This is important so that we can avoid even attempts to establish deep relationships with those who conflict with values we hold dear and are not willing to compromise. If we do not know our core values, and are in the process of discovering them during relationships, we may appear to be immature at best and schizophrenic at worst, when actions by others trigger what would appear to be massively disproportionate reactions from us, because we suddenly realize that their actions conflict with the very fibers of our emotional, physical or spiritual components.

Compatibility

In order to have harmonious relationships, we must seek to emphasize those attributes that we have in common with others around us with whom we need to interact. With close personal relationships it behooves us to take the view that we are travelers who are making the conscious decision to share our space and resources while on this journey. We should take the view that we are traveling in the same wagon with these chosen individuals through both good times and bad, as we travel to a common destination or for the period that we share the journey. As such, prior to embarking on this shared journey, we must take the time to review what baggage each party adds to the wagon, and we need to determine what duties each will provide for the duration of the voyage. We must be flexible but this will serve to clarify expectations and responsibilities.

We need to acknowledge that each party has had their independent journeys up to this point in time, and has accumulated their share of "baggage". Some of that baggage may have to be left behind simply because the wagon can only progress forward with a set maximum load or some of the baggage that passengers may want to take on the journey may be disruptive and cause disharmony with others on the wagon. Remember, all do not have to climb onto the same wagon! Those who insist on taking absolutely all their stuff may indeed need their own wagons! They may not have the sincere desire to, or may not have the self-control needed to compromise, and thus share a common space with others, resulting in them not being very good companions for any extended periods.

Honesty in communicating our expectations for the duration of the common journey is very important. As we travel with others, it is also important to note that we all have the powers of discerning much about our companions. As we explore and develop ourselves, we become more aware, and if we trust our instincts, we can have a very good idea of what the strengths and weaknesses of our fellow travelers.

Although this may sound a bit trite, in order to make optimal progress in any one direction, it is very important that those who pull the wagon, pull in the same direction! This should be applied with diligence to how we care for our most precious possessions i.e. health and relationships, in the quality of the foods we consume and the values we hold dear and which we will not compromise. This also holds true in our current societies to the manner in which we deal with our finances.

In order to maintain successful relationships, we need to recognize that we are not clones. We each have our own set of God (ok, I said it!) given talents, and in order to develop the strongest relationships, similar to developing children, we must tap into the strengths of everyone involved in the relationship. This is an effort that not all may have to be involved to the same degree, in every activity, and yet everyone contributes to the best of their ability and for benefit of all involved. As an example: whoever is best at cooking takes the lead and dictates to everyone else what their duties will be. This also apples to finances, cleaning, and just about every task which has to be completed in both daily routine activities, as well as in exceptional situations. This allocating of duties allows each participant to feel fulfilled and rewarded for being able to contribute. By enabling each individual to serve, we are contributing to them fulfilling their spiritual need,. All this can occur while allowing others to learn to work in multiple capacities, such as both lead and team members, as well as learn to have the discipline required to give kudos to whomever provides leadership. Thus, the values of sharing and service are constantly being reinforced, encouraged and rewarded.

Here is another way of looking at something that introduced earlier: relationship circles. Consider each participant in a relationship as a circle. Within the relationship harmony is achieved when the circles overlap, and the more overlap there is, the more compatible we are. However, two circles will almost never have a one hundred percent overlap, so we must be aware that there will always be an disparities which are those areas that do not overlap. In order to maintain harmony, areas that do not overlap must not cause conflict with the core values of the other party, else we run the risk of shrinking the overlap until... well, conflict will be a major component of the relationship while it lasts!

These examples might serve to make this principle clearer. Two individuals are planning to share their lives journeys together, one party however, has certain habits or friends that really conflict with some of the core values of the other partner (stealing, drugs, infidelity, you add your own!)./In order to reduce the stress in the relationship and on the wagon, it must be made clear that some baggage just has to go!. Because of the significance of harmony versus stress on the wagon, which as we know may start with one issue, but tends to spill over into other areas, it would be best to throw this piece of baggage out, so that the parties on the journey can achieve more harmony. As with all things, we need to be aware that when we make these demands, they must not be based in selfishness where we care only about ourselves instead of truly attempting to improve the quality of the relationship. Another version of this same theme can be applied when selecting partners in a business relationship. Certain traits, such as distrust or cheating, must never be allowed to ride on the wagon, as these traits will always lead to negative, stressful situations which will almost always degrade the quality of the relationship.

By recognizing the strengths of every party in a relationship and requesting their contributions, we create win/win/win situations. This means that you, I and others, who though they may simply observe, can learn and benefit from then manner in which we conduct our relationships. We create relationships that thrive and are examples to all with whom we come in contact.

Relationships are complicated. Mastery is making the complicated look easy. There are certain attributes that must be present and there are others whose presence makes it difficult, if not impossible, to establish or maintain good relationships. One such detrimental ingredient which we must strive to control and even eliminate is selfishness. In order for a relationship to grow, it must have contributions from the involved parties, selfishness strains all relationships.

Oftentimes we must give that which we want most, in order to make that component a part of our relationship. By introducing this formerly absent attribute we make it a part of, and eventually something that we may get out of the relationship. This is true of affection, words of encouragement, and so many more benefits that we may want out of our relationships! As an example, if we want our children, partners (spouses or business) to be happy and responsive to our desires, we should practice providing them with something which they find pleasant. That something may be as simple as kind words, or, we may in fact introduce unexpected qualities, this way, we give more than is expected. This is also true when we show real appreciation or concern for someone when that quality is not expected, such as in a business relationship. By giving more than is expected, many times we will find that people respond to us regardless of whether or not they are conscious of their reaction, and we may in fact bring out qualities in these individuals that others may not be aware that these qualities exists. This may enrich us to the extent that we discover enough about others, through what would normally be fleeting, casual encounters that allow us to make the conscious choice to move them from one of our outer circles to our closer inner circles.

When we are aware of our core values and detect individuals who conflict with these values, we can have relationships with them, but, we must be careful to relegate these individuals to the outer circles, instead of those circles reserved for those whom we hold near and dear. Based on the preceding, it should be apparent that we can in fact have relationships with every individual. What changes is that we consciously designate circles with ourselves at the center and attach relationships to a circle at varying distances from ourselves. Along with the distance that we assign to these circles, will be associated rules of trust and conduct to be observed with those we allow into our respective circles. Thus, we can have those with whom we associate based on common business interests, but with whom we by the nature of our interactions are always in competition, relegated to positions that are not as close as those who share a lot in common with us at much deeper emotional, physical and even spiritual levels.

Relationship mentors

If we want to have our best relationships possible, besides improving our understanding of ourselves and the individuals with whom we must interact, there are no greater assets than those we choose as mentors for our relationships. It is extremely important that we understand the significance of choosing the right individuals, when we seek advice on conducting the affairs of our relationships. Since good relationships are one of our most valuable possessions, we must seek others who have experience in the types of relationships in which we are involved. This is a very important point: we must admire the manner in which they have conducted their affairs in their own relationships. We must not take advice on financial matters from those who we can observe do have positive experiences with their own finances. The same rule applies for seeking advice on dealing with our offspring: if we do not admire someone else's children we should not follow their advice or opinion if we want to have success in raising our own children. By the same token, if we seek advice or mentoring for our personal relationships, we should seek those who have long- term success in their relationships. Preferably the answers we seek will be obtained from others within our families or culture.

Worse than any lack of knowledge is our reliance on the advice of others have only demonstrated the ability to cultivate bad relationships. This is almost a guarantee of having unpleasant outcomes, and thus undesirable baggage on our life journeys. The preponderance of individuals who have one or more divorces and the affiliated negative experiences, who serve as advisers and confidants to us when we are dealing with uncertainties or other issues in our relationships, tend to lead us towards the same unpleasant or unproductive outcomes that they experienced.

One method that we could all apply in our journey is at all times to take a "village view" (see appendix of the "village view principle") of anyone who is dispensing advice to us in our personal or professional affairs. In short, we must not follow but rather choose to ignore the advice of anyone who has not demonstrated the principles that they espouse. If we follow this simple "village view" principle, many of our negative experiences based on ill-advised actions will be avoided.

In order to get the most and best out of those whom we allow in our inner circles, we should seek foremost to assist them in developing all their components (i.e. the emotional, physical and spiritual), so that they can accomplish whatever tasks they set for themselves. They will also be able to serve as sources of strength if we ever need emotional, physical or spiritual support. Thus, by giving we are in fact enabling others so that we become part of a stronger group. No family, business or military will succeed in the long term if led by a strong leader but comprised of emotional, physical and spiritual weaklings!

Whatever we may build will continue to thrive, if we teach and demonstrate by example the value of personal growth and the development of the inner strength to all in our inner circle. This strength is a result of balancing the development of our inner components. As we seek to develop ourselves and share these methods, we will become incredibly richer, as we enable and foster stronger and more meaningful relationships.

SECTION III

CULTURE AND SOCIETY

SOCIETIES, WHAT THRIVES?

A society is as strong as the principles it is based upon and the adherence of all it's citizens to those principles. When those principles give all members a sense of security, belonging, fairness and provides opportunities for the growth and development for all of its citizens, the society will thrive. If however, the guiding principles enshrine rules that do not garner the respect of all its citizens, the principles enshrined in that foundation document will be worn away like the stone against a river. As a consequence, the respect necessary to maintain the preeminence of the doctrine will be lacking, and conformity will be replaced by derision, which leads to challenges and the eventual removal of that which represents the foundation stone of the society.

All members must demonstrate reverence to those principles enshrined in that document. If leaders place themselves above the tenets of that doctrine, in time citizens will also place themselves outside the boundaries of it's domain. It is therefore important that the constitution of a society is based on values that embody permanence and recognition of principles that preserve the rights of the individual, and encourage the development of all members, so that regardless of the heritage of any of its citizens, it adds to the value of individuals, families, and thus to the entire society. As with any organism or form of organization, the guidelines of its existence should be conducive to not only its self- preservation, but should also be conducive to continued propagation.

Every society should be governed by rules that strengthen its citizens and foster behaviors that lead to cohesiveness among individuals and efficiency in the usage of all resources.

Down through recorded time we have had several different forms of government to maintain our societies, and almost all societies are structured after some form of pyramidal design. As with real pyramids, each part is connected to and dependent on another part in order for the pyramid to maintain its structure and integrity. Efficient systems place top priority on maintaining the integrity of the system. In case of our societies this normally means establishing a balance between the power and influence of those who reside at the top of the pyramid, normally the administrators, and those whose actions provide the basis of the society, which is normally the working class whose activities provide most of the basic products and services on which the entire society thrives.

Enlightened leaders can prolong the life of our societal pyramids by ensuring that those who reside at the top of the societal pyramid are not being much of a burden to those below them. Those who comprise the base of our societal pyramids must be just as engaged in the distribution of products and services as our administrators. Societies crumble when there is a disconnect between the apexes and bases of their systems, or when those at the top become too burdensome to the base. Our societies rise and fall based on this simple principle. We should devise systems that maintain this equilibrium through efficiency

In times past monarchies or derivatives were the pre-eminent form of government, monarchies, that were connected to and created a bond with the 'common' people, thrived. When generations passed after the monarchy has been established and power had passed down to heirs who no longer recognized the relationship between the top and base of the societal pyramid, often these leaders became alienated, and often opposed to working for the benefit of anyone but themselves. These disconnected monarchs then disqualified themselves from being in power as *none is qualified to have power over those they despise*. Eventually, their military forces were turned against those whom they should have been protecting. Eventually this almost always led to the eventual overthrow of the tyrant monarch and the destruction of the societal pyramid.

Because of men's obsession with power, incipient greed and the lack of enlightenment by leaders, communism has largely gone the same path, and by the same method. Even democracy which has the benefit of not suppressing the human spirit and allowing for the creativity of any of its' citizens will slowly be eroded, until in many instances, it is democracy in name only. For in many places those at the top of the societal pyramid will find deceitful methods to hold onto power in spite of the will of the majority.

To this end, it will become obvious that in time the most popular system of government -democracy- is not tenable when coupled with unbridled greed. Because of the coupling of finances and the mechanics of democracy those elected are constantly being unduly influenced by the richest individuals and therefore the elected are prone to serve primarily those who have the most. Those who have the most in a greed- based system often have very little or no concern for those who have less -except to the extent of trying to be merchants to them- and they may even be contemptuous of the needs and aspirations of the underclass. This leads to a downward spiral where the lower classes become more oppressed and cannot trust their elected politicians because regardless of their participation in the democratic process, their needs may not be addressed.

Since these lower classes tend to be the most populous, in time, the upper classes and the elected politicians will devise strategies to minimize the effect of the lower classes through special qualifications or outright exclusions, thereby invalidating the concept of democracy by excluding much of the masses of the society. One scenario which leads to the diminishing of democracy is as follows: through greed, which is the worst attribute of any society, those who have power at all levels of society; whether that be in the political or the business realm, concentrate wealth for themselves at the expense of, and with contempt for those who are lower down in the respective pyramids. In the initial stages, those at the top of these pyramids may have an understanding of the relationship with the base of the pyramids that they govern. Over time however, their successors, who may not have been properly educated in the dynamics involved, eventually become disqualified to govern based on their ignorance and the resulting contempt for the working class base of the pyramid.

Since the base of any pyramid has the benefits of numbers, in a true democracy, in time, the base will have power through those who may rise up from these working classes as sons and daughters of the often oppressed or simply overlooked lower classes. This phenomenon of the working classes choosing leaders who are opposed to the usual ruling elite will only be possible in, and thus, will be native to societies that have embraced the concept of democracy. In time however, the ruling elite will devise methods to ensure that the transference of power to the masses is not solely based on the sheer numbers of the population. Some of the methods involved will be systematic disqualification of entire sections of the populations' ability to participate in the democratic system, i.e. disqalifiy many from the right to vote., as well as devising methods of using proxies for individuals to ensure that simply a majority of the population is not sufficient, but a majority of the proxy, which can be manipulated by laws. In time however, as the disconnect between the apex and base becomes more pronounced, more effort will be required by the ruling classes to ensure their continued dominance.

Eventually, there will be multiple instances of democracies whose leaders are popularly elected, however, their election will create severe discomfort for other democratically elected leaders, based on their opposing alignment with the policies of those who historically have been at the base of society and other leaders whose policies are geared towards those who have traditionally formed the apex. In other words, if special qualifications and exclusions are not successful, the phenomena of democratically elected governments, which are unpopular with the upper classes, will become more predominant. This has already started to occur in the early twenty first century in countries such as Venezuela, Bolivia, Haiti etc.

This phenomenon is not new: from the rise and fall of monarchies, to communism, these systems all fail due to the disconnect created when over generations, unbridled greed infiltrates the ruling classes. This results in the disconnect between those who labor and create the products on which the society thrives, and those who do not create, but due to their wealth, control the system for their benefits with contempt for the wellbeing of the producer class. This phenomena is analogous to a pyramid in which the apex is contemptuous of its base and through its folly and arrogance does not recognize or seek to learn about how much its prominence and very existence is dependent on the proliferation of everything beneath itself.

This disconnect is already very apparent in most corporations. Those at the helm are already becoming contemptuous of those who are at the base of these profit pyramids, so much so that as their benefits are becoming completely detached from the compensation of any of their workers. Regardless of the fact that they may have all their needs met for hundreds of years based on their total earnings, the leaders because they are driven by greed continue to take as much as is possible, even adding more to themselves while dispossessing their workers, often in the name of efficiency!

The common denominator in all the failures of the various forms of governments is the overarching weaknesses of the chosen leaders. Monarchies, communism, democracy and any other form of government are as strong as those who lead. When we have leaders who are ignorant of the bonds which hold the society together, their action may place intense stresses on these bonds. Over time the weaknesses of the leaders, and often their actions, which erode the founding principles, will tend to permeate the society. As such, the existence of "crackdowns on corruption" are indeed an indictment of current or past leaders. In time even the very foundation units of the society, the family, may be splintered and weakened, leaving the entire society with cracks at its very foundation. At this point all demonstrations of solidarity become ceremonial but not heartfelt, as most individuals will be committed to emulate their selfish leaders, seeking to obtain for themselves by any means the maximum power and physical possessions. Any desire to work towards a shared vision of the future, is replaced by a selfish desire, regardless of possible negative consequences for anyone else including the larger society.

The most destructive attribute a society can foster is greed, and the worst attitude is conceit.

Societies that encourage conceit by its citizens will in time find, that the ability to grow through the acquisition of knowledge will be stymied, for much of our growth comes from observing and asking objective questions about that which is outside ourselves. Conceit can blind us to the benefits to be derived from the people, plants, animals and cultures we encounter. Conceit prevents us from having an open mind about things we do not understand. Conceit allows us to have only a slanted view of what we observe, thus, conceit renders us incapable of seeking real answers to the currently unexplained. It is conceit which results in us subjecting those who would ask questions or pose theories about observed but not understood phenomenon to ridicule. Much of our advances in the sciences, which enrich our lives daily, are a result of dogged research by dedicated and determined individuals. These advances occur often in spite of derision and ridicule by many of the conceited 'scholars' of the day. There have been many 'experts' who have been declaring emphatically for many centuries that we have explained all that is explainable. This trend continues even today, as our current experts in most fields would state that they understand everything and the inner workings of every process that exists. However, if we look back through history, we will find that these statements have been made before, and in time revelations prove that our knowledge is constantly expanding. Thus, many of the theories that have been advanced are in fact incomplete works that often hold errors or critical omissions… We must remember that research in spite of conceited 'scholars' have enabled us to progress past such beliefs as a flat earth being the center of the universe, the benefits of margarine as compared to butter and the total lack of purpose of the appendix.

It is important to note here that all our scientific knowledge from medicine to computerization is based on the discoveries of devoted individuals, and the realization of principles which have existed since the beginning of time as we know it. The purpose of stating this obvious fact is to recognize that we do not create internal processes or new forces, we simply discover these processes or the mechanics of their operation and learn to harness these forces Yet, we continue to foster conceit which prevents us from even acknowledging that things that are not currently understood exist, sometimes despite incontrovertible proof of their existence. Skepticism can be healthy, conceit is almost always counterproductive.

Influences and effects

Healthy societies should seek to ensure that the most influential support groups for individuals are their immediate families. Every society, that seeks to be prosperous and establish a culture worth preserving through time, is based on the support of families and individuals. Close families can provide support and corrective pressures when needed to ensure that individuals conform to norms based on their cultural traditions. Societies may benefit from breaking these strong bonds so detached individuals are encouraged to become more susceptible to behaviors that benefit the society, Yet, any benefit from these short- term actions will be detrimental to the preservation of the culture in the long- term. Such is the case of systems based on greed. Greed is a scourge, greed will destroy the fabric of any society. Families that may have had close bonds for many generations or even centuries can be destroyed by the infiltration of greed.

By persuading the most emotional individuals to believe that the achievement of physical items will lead to the fulfillment of their emotional needs, greed can be introduced into any group. Thus those who seek the normal emotional bliss associated with acceptance and adulation are most vulnerable to this type of manipulation. Information indicating that the acquisition of some product or service will somehow transform them into more beautiful or more desirable individuals than their current perception of themselves can create an obsessive desire in these weak individuals. As a result, the weak capitulate to the mechanisms of those who market these products and services by using these manipulative methods.

If however, this type of advertising is pitched to individuals who are balanced in their internal components, they would be less likely to be influenced into becoming victims of those who may choose to prey on the weak, with their pitches to purchase products which they know provide only fleeting emotional fulfillment. These balanced individuals would be able to resist, because they presumably surround themselves with real circles of individuals from which they receive their emotional fulfillment, instead of yearning to have this need met by unknown parties.

Much of the same results can be observed if fear, i.e. fear of some threat or fear of loss, is used by any merchandiser, instead of the desire to be loved and admired. Greed can be the motivation of people outside the group to attempt to prey on group members. However it is also just as common and more detrimental when this greed originates within the group. Does anyone have to be reminded that where there is greed, there will not be transparency and thus there cannot be trust? Unfortunately this most debasing vice is often encouraged in the business world.

Most businesses are governed by rules established by government, and most businesses seek to be profitable. This profit, however, very often is concentrated in the hands of the few at the top of the pyramid. While this uneven distribution may be the reward for the visionary work and the risks assumed by those who lead these companies, oftentimes as these business entities mature, those who assume the leadership positions may have very little to do with the risks of establishing the business. More importantly, as with the demise of all social pyramidal structures, because these individuals may not have had any connection with those who labored at the base of these pyramids, in time these leaders very often seek to disenfranchise many breadwinning individuals and thus families, due to greed. This disenfranchisement may be concurrent with leaders extravangantly enriching themselves while using buzzwords such as productivity and efficiency to justify or as cover for their negative actions. Very often the increases in benefits that these leaders, who are not in financial need, grant themselves could more than defray the cost of supporting the beneficial relationships between the business enterprises and laid -off employees.

A more efficient, rewarding and self-sustaining model for all business enterprises in any society is the reinvestment of profits into families and individuals. Thus, emphasis should not only be placed on the benefits of core stakeholder, but also on the simple measure of how many families are supported by the continued operation of the business. Instead of only focusing on generating profit from the operations of the business, equally important is the numbers of individuals or families who benefit not only from the products or services provided, but also from the numbers of individuals or families that benefit from the efficient operation of the business. If we would use these premises as the primary reasons for the operation of any business, instead of only the generation of profits for a small group of individuals, we would provide more opportunities for more individuals to be involved in generating benefits from the existence of all our industries. Besides benefits to the society at large, every business should be required to be efficient. Efficient businesses would achieve the maximum productivity possible for their investment in resources. It would be very difficult for competition to overtake these businesses, as their operational costs would make it untenable for inefficient competition, as well as their relationships with customers would be irreplaceable.

Based on the above principles, small businesses may support only a limited number of families, but if they are efficient, they will challenge any other even larger businesses, and so in time, based on the increased revenues and profits generated, benefit larger percentages of the society. Especially effected would be those who are directly involved in the operation of the business, as they will realize increased benefits from the efficient operation and growth of the business.

This would ensure that riches in a society are distributed to the core units that make up that society, and that the natural pyramids in our societies have support at all levels. By demanding that every individual contribute to some level as required, business enterprises would foster ingenuity and the growth of human potential, ensuring wherever possible, that prosperity should be tied to performance. Performance should be measured based on results and not weighed based on factors not directly related to that performance.

Support for individuals and families means providing the resources that strengthen, not curtail the abilities of individuals in favor of governmental supports. Governments should provide the services that enable all members of society to develop themselves through self-control and awareness so that individuals become more responsible for their actions. Most irresponsible actions of the young are related to irresponsibility in their nurturing environment. A society that teaches vision and self-control gives each individual and family a sense of purpose, not just the ability to react to what happens in the present, but also the ability to sustain their actions with a focus on future objectives as well as cultural directives.

Teaching self-control and vision will enable each proponent to become enlightened. As a consequence, these teachings can result in the suppression of drug addiction, teenage pregnancies, high rates of school dropouts and other irresponsible behaviors.

Balanced individuals attract and maintain circles that provide all the support needed by the individuals, and most people, when made aware, will chose actions which do not degrade but will be beneficial to their futures.

Efficiency and sustainability versus greed

There are two principles every individual, family, business, culture and group should be aware of, and seek to incorporate into all activities: strive to be efficient and ensure that all critical actions are sustainable. Most of our failures can be attributed to lack of conformance to these two principles. This is usually cased by a lack of awareness, which in itself is attributable to not being efficient, as real efficiency accounts for all known issues related to any operation. Nature gives us many examples of adherence to these principles without the greed that normally is a part of most human systems. As individuals, we are each models of sustainability and efficiency.

Efficiency and sustainability should be the core principles of our societies. Understanding and striving to be efficient, as well as ensuring sustainability are beneficial abilities to the individual, culture, every group and the society. One might think that not only would our societies encourage and place priority on the teaching these principles. One might also imagine that there would be active deterrents to the proliferation of systems that conflict with these principles.

Individuals, businesses and societies. who ignore the principles of efficiency and sustainability may thrive, but any prosperity will nonetheless still be governed by these principles. As such, events governed by greed tend to foster inefficient activities which are only sustainable for some finite time period. In most, if not all our systems, greed is the factor that causes us to ignore these two governing principles and as such, most of our current systems are prone to imprudent actions, which in time adversely affect those who are dependent on them.

Systems based on efficiency propagate the growth, development and proliferation of the system by ensuring that the needs of all essential parts of the system are met – every part works for the benefit of other parts, our bodies are models of this efficiency. Systems based on greed tend towards their own destruction through the selfish actions of whatever part(s) that are dominant. In greed based systems dominant components are allowed to 'choke the life' out of other parts which may be essential, by concentrating benefits in one area while systematically depriving others. Greed based systems may generate efficiencies by their actions but, efficiency is not an objective nor is it a priority. Efficiency seeks to ensure sustainability, greed does not.

The Foundation Blocks

Most societies decay as a result of being governed by unenlightened individuals who are most interested in the power of the state as a proxy for their own power. Over time, these leaders impose laws which strip away the power of, and invade the sanctity of individuals and families, thereby effectively weakening the building blocks of the society.

The ultimate achievement of the spiritual component is service. If our leaders are balanced and enlightened individuals, we will all be able to recognize the sacrifices that our leaders make on behalf of those they lead. Since many in a society emulate the actions of the most powerful or influential, enlightened leaders can lead to an enlightened populace. If however the leaders are consumed by greed and the acquisition of power, this greed will be modeled in the society. This can increase the stresses between groups and individuals, until in the latter stages of our societies, we will experience more and more demonstrations of leaders who are threatened by the proliferation of the values they embody, using their military to target the people who the military should have been created to defend. As leaders see their leadership as a function of power and not of service, we will witness the escalation of wars, since they view their personal agendas as more important than the needs of their citizens. This escalation cannot go on forever, as there are always compensating factors that will always serve to quell or extinguish these leaders' ambitions.

Services should be provided to every family who may be having difficulties to reinforce the bond between family members. Men and women should be reminded of their respective roles within the families, and should be reminded that their vision and actions are vitally important to the degree of success and continuity of culture imparted to every member of their family unit. It is in the interest of every society to disseminate that knowledge needed for the execution of roles vital to the benefit of the society. To this end, educational materials and opportunities should be presented to the public on matters that affect the lives of all in the society. These educational materials should include health, legal and financial information to empower every individual. Vision and self-control should also be encouraged to assist in the personal development of all who are willing to undergo the relevant training.

Every society should provide counseling to those members whose actions seem to be detrimental to the normal functioning of the various groups that comprise the building blocks of the society. Those who govern should strive to put services in place that enable the strengthening of not only individuals, but every family. Family education should stress the traditional roles played by each member of the family, as well as raising the awareness that many of these traditional roles may be sharable. For example, men can cook, clean and care for their children, and women can be builders and providers. This education should seek to remind everyone that the ultimate goal is the sharing the burden of "pulling the wagon" and in order to have the strongest family unit, each member must contribute based on his or her ability.

Society should foster innovation and strive to bring out the talents of every member, as this serves the greater good of the community.

Social services should always include education that strengthens individuals, and reinforce the values that strengthen families. They should also raise awareness of the daily functioning of various aspects of the society. For example, this could be done by providing a series of "how to" manuals, that show examples of how to save, use credit, and provide healthy nutrition.

Societies should encourage the teachings of culture because therein lies the source of family strength and unity. All individuals should be made aware that the society is as strong as the sum of all its citizens, and by seeking to grow strong, each individual is making the society stronger.

Self-control is always based of one's views of oneself, and the more a vision of the future is incorporated into this picture, the more responsibility is taught to individuals. This personal responsibility model is not taught in most societies because many in power desire to influence and ultimately control the will of others, failing to realize that by strengthening individuals and families, they actually strengthen the society. We will only achieve our potential as a society when we have progressed to the point where we realize the value of vision and self-control and ensure that the teaching of both disciplines is made available to all citizens.

Many of the vices that weaken the fibers of a society are based in the lack of fulfillment of individuals. Much of this lack of fulfillment is a result of the young being taught that their individual value is based on how they are viewed by others. In families that have a strong connection to an established culture and strong bonds between family members, each member's behavior is somewhat tailored by the expectations of other members. While this is a sound basis for the continuation of the culture, it may not be optimal and so each individual should learn to assimilate information from the source that provides the strongest leadership by example. This may be from within the family or from the larger culture and society.

In a society where others outside the family have a desire to influence the decisions of the family or individual members of the family for the benefit of these outside interests, there may be concerted attempts to divide and conquer families. Examples of this can be seen by merchants who want individuals to purchase new items on a regular basis, as in the annual purchase of seasonal items. Certain sectors of the culture create pressures based on the emotional need for acceptance and adulation to subtly coerce individuals to become bigger consumers and to propagate this pattern to their entire families even when this type of activity conflicts with their traditional values.

Through advertising, the emotional are led to believe that they would be viewed by others outside their immediate family circles as not being 'fashionable', assuming their immediate family is not already influenced by this behavior, and thus those who obsessively seek acceptance are led to believe that they will not receive the adulation that is associated with being 'in fashion.'

It is in the interest of many merchants to 'break' the bond of family where it is necessary to pry members away from family traditions and into the service of the merchants and all the ancillary services like other merchants and credit. This weakens individuals overall self-control and makes them more responsive to their emotional needs. Thus begins a downward spiral of seeking the next action to achieve short term happiness, with no vision or concern for long term negative consequences. This pattern can be seen in the children who grew up in homes where the parents have succumbed to simply being 'super consumers' who very often become delinquent in responding to their children emotional or spiritual needs and fail to provide hugs, kind words, encouragement, acceptance/adulation and have instead chosen to pamper them with physical objects.

One of the most detrimental side effects of this behavior manifests itself in their children, who as little sponges lose any connection to prior cultural habits and adopt the only behavioral patterns to which they are exposed. Thus an entire generation can be raised with their only sense of self-worth tied to things totally external to themselves! These items can be as simple as certain brands of footwear, clothing, jewelry, cars or living in a certain neighborhood. Even the fundamentals of their physical beings, like healthy eating habits and working, within even close family relationships can be severely compromised to the extent that there are no longer close bonds between relatives, such as cousins or even siblings.

It is a tragedy indeed when a society replaces the need for an individual's self-control and self-discipline with professionals whose job functions are to who cater to, and support the continued weakening of many. Thus, many behaviors that can be curbed by the self-control of individuals become the basis for industries that thrive by treating the symptoms as diseases that must be managed by professionals. Complicity for profit by these professionals may serve to perpetrate the actions of these individuals and may hasten the breakdown of the family unit. Societies can arrest and reverse the breakdown of families by making the teachings of vision and self-control available to all.

When individuals, families and societies are dominated by their emotional needs, there is increased vulnerability to chart a course that can lead to destruction, caused by the adoption of behaviors that satisfy the immediate and temporary needs instead of building strengths that serve throughout good and bad times.

Every individual, culture and society should strive to be efficient and sustainable. Much can and must be learnt from observing nature, and one of the disciplines that every successful society should embrace is to be as efficient as possible. In order to achieve this end, all members of a society should be taught as many efficiency practices as possible, and even laws should only be enacted if they are not counterproductive to an efficient system.

We have realized many benefits of building systems based on the rules of nature. And if we do focus on these rules of nature, these systems can be very efficient. Oftentimes however, industries find ways to keep driving up the price of these benefits to the masses due to greed, although thanks to internal efficiencies their costs for providing these benefits are greatly reduced. As of the writing of this book, we have begun to harness the potential of sound, light, magnetism and other forces of nature. Yet, since our systems are dominated by males, these revelations of nature's forces are almost always first deployed in the pursuit of power.

Therefore, there are some forces that we may be precluded from harnessing due to the potentially immensely detrimental effects we could have on others if these forces were placed at our disposal. These discoveries will occur only after we have become so enlightened that we no longer place a priority on attaining power through the destruction of others. Imagine the following scenario for a moment: if we had the same capability of harnessing the power of light with the forces that constitute gravity What would be the equivalents of creating light through electricity, of adjusting the lighting, of breaking light into it's components and using them for our benefits (IR/UV etc), of concentrating light into lasers, of harnessing light to create electricity? At least our mode of transportation as well as ideas on the current limits we place on our ability to traverse large distances would need a complete overhaul. In our current state however, this capability would most likely find itself being deployed in the destruction of others, as it would undoubtedly be first be used in the military to deploy destructive devices in the name of future prosperity!

Enlightened systems will be based on efficiency. Nature is based on efficiency, and although we may not view many natural processes as humane, they are efficient. As in nature, competition in efficient systems is based on ability – we can achieve this efficiency in our educational system where all would be tested and the best qualified regardless of the ability to pay for services would be granted the opportunity to pursue further education at the most prestigious schools. Consequently, regardless of their background or upbringing, the most skilled are afforded the opportunity to advance so that society benefits from its most talented individuals. In a truly progressive society, everyone will be given opportunities based on their abilities.

Greed based societies will not allow unlimited social mobility but will seek instead to keep in place a system of social classes. While this works in the short- term because those who initially made up the upper classes understood the connection between themselves and lower classes who provide the services, within generations their offspring may only have contempt for the lower classes. In time this contempt leads to conflicts, and when the lower classes reach a certain critical mass, pivotal incidents tend to lead to the destruction of the upper classes. Greed therefore works against itself by its unnaturally insatiable appetite and lack of regard for the other components necessary to maintain the harmonious balance needed to maintain a system in perpetuity.

The concept of providing opportunity to the best qualified can ensure that we create efficient systems, as opposed to systems based on greed. The qualifications of leaders in efficient systems would include a demonstrated ability to care for those whom they seek to lead. They would also demonstrate vision and self-control, so that critical decisions that affect the future are forward- looking to ensure the continuation of the system with harmony between all components of the system. Like a tree planted in fertile soil with an ample supply of nutrients needed to sustain itself gives back more by way of products and byproducts (oxygen, fruits, decaying leaves etc.), good leaders not only thrive, but seek to give back to ensure the continued prosperity of all their constituents.

While it may or may not be possible to change anyone, prosperous societies should place a priority on providing services which strengthen individuals and families, and seek less to destroy these units or their basic human rights. This work is an attempt to not only inform of the detrimental attributes of most societies but also an attempt to seek to provide methods for personal enlightenment and enriching all relationships, so that families can reap the significant benefits associated with enlightened members.

The importance of vision to those who lead cannot be stressed enough. Individuals, families, businesses and entire societies falter and may face ruination due to a lack of vision by their leaders.

Individuals who have an awareness of the perils of conceit, a thirst for the accumulation of knowledge and understanding, are likely to become cornerstones in the foundation of a strong and persevering society. They should be unfettered and encouraged.

By fostering an environment of learning without conceit, any culture or society will be stronger because of the contributions of talents by all the diverse members of the community. True super powers will always harness the talents of all the world's diverse peoples and cultures. Differences in cultures bring different points of view and different ways of looking at situations. These differing viewpoints will often result in novel solutions to societal challenges.

Cultures and societies are stronger, more efficient and sustainable when they seek to strengthen and develop every individual to their maximum potential. Many societies, instead, are more concerned with developing a few individuals, and forcing compliance on the majority through the implementation of laws based on hypocrisy. These laws may serve to limit freedoms and ultimately the development of the human spirit. These laws are often selectively enforced and disproportionably applied across various groups.

Our civilization will be trapped in a cycle of renewal until we get past the notion of superiority and embrace our differences and seek to harness the capabilities and strengths of each group. We choose to go through this phase, due to our insistence on the execution of this unfortunate series of events, we will only advance to a true age of enlightenment upon its completion.

We should all be mindful of the lessons of history. It is conceit for the lessons of experience which causes us to repeat past failures. We must seek to emulate those characteristics we admire and recognize that the fate of our societies will depend largely on the leaders we choose.

As members of our societies, we should be aware of the primary qualities required by anyone who desires to lead. As such, we should be vigilant in selecting only leaders who honor the following principles: they honor knowledge and science, they have vision, they demonstrate self-control and they delight in diversity. We must all be mindful that we do not devolve from caring for the individual to minding the state, or placing anything else above the care of the individual.

SECTION IV

IMPROVING, ADAPTING

THE BIG PICTURE – BE GOAL ORIENTED!

If you have taken the time to read this far, you should be reading everything that follows with this in mind: this is about you, not your parents, relatives, friends or acquaintances. This is not about anything you may own or anything that is external to you. This is about you and as such there is no need to speak with anyone except to seek assistance with your understanding of concepts or for possible future mentoring. The objective of this section is to provide real guidance to assist you in becoming stronger so that you can gain more self-control, enabling you to be in a position to assist others. This is about you becoming stronger, being able to cope better, having a better understanding of what makes others behave the way they do, and as such enable you to make those subtle adjustments to bring out the best in those you encounter. This should enable you to replace conceit with a thirst for knowledge and a desire to understand as well as teach you how to obtain the strength to perform those actions ("close the gap") that cause positive changes in your health and all your relationships, as those are your two most precious possessions.

We all should aspire to be the very best we can be, in order to maximize our talents, to bring out the very best in all whom we encounter and to achieve the pinnacle of success based on our abilities, we must first learn self-control. With self-control we become lights that shine on all that is around us and examples to all who are blessed to share our existence. Self-control is not achieved by talking to others about ourselves; we may seek external help to understand our reactions to external stimuli, or to seek guidance in controlling these reactions.

We can only achieve conscious self-control if we have a sincere desire to have self-control, and are prepared to follow a discipline of introspection and exercises to strengthen our will and enhance our vision so that we can implement our vision of ourselves in all our activities.

The key to controlling anything is to first understand that thing which we are trying to control. It is no different with ourselves, we must have the will to perform an honest and thorough self-examination in order to have an understanding of ourselves. At the very outset, this may seem like somewhat of an overwhelming task, but you can use this book as both a starting point and a guide for performing this most important function.

This is about our lives and experiences as individuals, each of us is different although we have quite a lot in common. Our experiences may be similar, but our reactions can vary to the extremes, so it is important in a self- examination to precisely confine our analysis to our own experiences and reactions. Therefore, having the input of others on what we feel is obviously not productive, since they must interpret what they think we feel. Requesting outside input or feedback on how to react to these feelings is another matter and depends on each individual's personal needs.

In order to be productive, we must have goals, our goals enable us to be focused on the tasks we must perform. We must also learn to incorporate milestones along the way to achieving our objectives. Milestones are those imaginary points we place on the way to our destination, so that we can measure our progress. Since most of the exercises provided here are about self-control and eventual self-improvement, we need to be able to set individual goals and milestones, so that we can check our own progress. As an example, the first thing we need to aware of and control is something that is essential to life itself and most take for granted, after all, it is automatic, that 'thing' is our breathing. When we get to the five step program, we will first need to control our breathing, our goal will be to both slow down our breathing and take deeper breaths. We can set our own time schedule or milestones to determine our progress towards our goal. We can view each accomplishment as a journey and we set our own milestones and periodically check to verify whether we have made the progress we intended when we started. So, if as is the intent of the breathing exercises we intend to take deep breaths that during inhalation last for at least five seconds and we are currently at say, two seconds inhalation, we can set a milestone of one, two or even three weeks by which time our normal inhalation time should have progressed from two to three seconds. These are our milestones we set for ourselves and so we should feel free to adjust them as necessary. However if we are to achieve our objectives and reap the rewards, we must keep pressing onwards towards our eventual goals.

This bears repeating: this is about you, and you consciously taking control of yourself, it is not about anyone controlling you or you controlling anyone or anything external to yourself. So unless you are in the habit of speaking to yourself, most of the techniques and exercises can and should be developed in silence. One of the objectives you should set for yourself is to become a master of self-control and you should eventually become adept at influencing events and people (note: not controlling!) based on your mastery of self, by the image you project to others.

Our two most valuable possessions are health and good relationships, many of our goals should be based on enhancing one of both of these treasures. Unlike trying to achieve wealth or power, health and good relationships depend on us constantly being aware of and looking out for ourselves, but not in a manner that makes us appear mean, selfish or arrogant.

To achieve the goal of good health, we must first recognize and acknowledge that every cell in our bodies is made from and fed by that which we put into our bodies. Recognize that food is not only essential but also a source of pleasure. We must therefore take the time to ensure that the foods we consume are of the best quality that we can afford. Over the long term, it makes no sense whatsoever to spend vast sums on those things that surround us, such as clothes, cars, houses etc. if we are not concerned with the quality of what we put into our bodies. Our bodies are very complex, but fortunately we do not have to know the details of all the intricate processes that are a part of us being healthy, even when we abuse our bodies over extended periods, our internal systems are always working to keep us in balance.

We should not be so conceited that we cannot learn, and we must not be so complacent or lazy that we abdicate from the responsibility to seek to expand our diets, so that all the raw materials needed for all the various processes in our bodies, are provided from excellent natural sources. Good health is more a product of what we eat than how much exercise we obtain, it should be obvious that our ability to perform as well as reap the benefits of exercise depends on what we eat. There are many volumes of information available on eating to maintain good health, we should take care though, to not follow conceited individuals who seek to profit from pigeon holing us into their narrow views of what is a healthy diet.

I would strongly suggest that we seek to expand our diets as much as possible, we should try to obtain all the known nutrients from as many different sources as are available. For example we should try to obtain our carbohydrates from tubers (yams, potatoes etc.), cereals (wheat, rice etc.) and vary these as much as is possible or we can afford. We should do the same for every ingredient that we put into our bodies. One of the benefits of expanding our diets is that we will introduce all the known, as well as currently unknown ingredients which serve as the building blocks or healing components to our bodies. We should think of eating as daily self- medication, and in time, with the advancement of knowledge, we will be able to introduce specific items into our diets to both combat diseases and degeneration, as well as promote or aid in the development of positive attributes such as alertness or changes to our metabolism.

We can set goals and milestones for achieving a healthier diet, we may first have to do some research into what types of foods provide the nutrients that we need and are available in our locale. We then would have to implement our plan of incorporating these new foods into our diets, as well as constantly looking for new ways to provide diverse building blocks to our bodies. With the inner strength that we develop as we increase our self- control, we will be able to perform conscious actions in order to meet our emotional, physical and spiritual needs. Because of the honesty we must develop when dealing with ourselves, we will no longer use masking agents or be in denial of our shortcomings or excesses that lead to long term ill health or recurring dysfunctional relationships.

Good relationships and health should be symbiotic treasures, with our elevated levels of consciousness, we can ensure that both health and good relationships are always served by our actions. Through our increased awareness we can radiate the qualities that we would like to have reflected back to us.

We must remember that those who perform actions, implement change. If we simply talk about change, but perform no actions, we may serve to initiate actions but, we are not implementing change and the nuances of the implementation may not be as we intended.

Our emotional needs are the most immediate that we should seek to examine in order to understand and possibly control. As you learn throughout the following pages and put these principles into practice, you will project yourself more admirably and be more influential to those with whom you come in contact. Once you ascertain what your core values are, and master the techniques for honing your vision and strengthening your willpower, you will be on the way to attaining the health and relationships that are truly enriching. With perseverance and diligence, you may eventually attain mastery of your spiritual, emotional and physical components and their associated needs. Mastery is the ability to make the complicated look easy!

In order to attain self-control, there are two attributes we need to develop, they are vision and willpower. Vision provides a point of focus and gives purpose to our actions. Willpower enables us to maintain that focus and to persevere until we achieve our goals. Before we delve into developing vision and strengthening our willpower however, we need to become familiar with this five step program which contains the techniques we will be employing throughout our development.

The following chapters will provide the methods by which you can improve these capabilities, and thus attain the abilities required to have a more fulfilling and rewarding existence. Your goal should be to build internal strength (physical, emotional and spiritual) so you can wean yourself of external support which does not return something to those who are giving support. As an analogy, you should aspire to grow strong bones and muscles, so you can stand independently and even help another instead of depending on the support of others. You must be prepared to do the work required to achieve results.

We may have physical impairments that hinder our progress or physical injuries which need to heal before we can perform certain tasks, but even more so than these physical challenges can be addressed, is the degree to which we can heal or repair any damage done to our emotional or spiritual components. It is the same with the growth we can attain in our emotional and spiritual components, if we have the vision and willpower to be persistent.

It is a natural that when we are young, we are dependent on others, and as we mature, we assume responsibilities that often require that we learn to share with, or provide for others. There are some however, who never fully attain maturation are solely concerned with acquiring, up to and until such time as their physical attributes are left behind at their transformation. We should all strive to reach the spiritual maturity that allows us to be of service to others.

Core Values

Our core values are those values that we hold so dear that they are part of the very foundation of our characters. These are the values that if compromised by anyone or any circumstance, we become very disturbed by the circumstances and uncomfortable, regardless of how close or distant we are to the individuals involved. Core values are personal values, they are integral parts of each of us, they are not simply values we would impose on, or simply want to observe in others. We must therefore build the strength to be representatives of those values so that we do not foster hypocrisy by our actions. Currently, our world is filled with hypocrisy, we can find many examples of leaders who demand that we do as they say, but not as they do.

Often our core values are tied to our component needs, and thus, to whichever component is dominant in our characters. Remember, the ultimate achievements of our emotional component is acceptance and adulation, our physical component it is power, and our spiritual component it is service and sacrifice. Our core values are not static. As we grow, information we receive may cause us to re-evaluate even our core values, even rebalancing our response to the needs of our various components can cause our core values to be adjusted. These changes take time however, and the stability of our core values are indeed a measure of the stability of our personality and character.

A determination of what are our core values can be accomplished by us reviewing our experiences to find which situations evoke both pleasant and unpleasant emotions, making a list of these emotions and the actions that stimulated those emotions, This can help us to pinpoint the values that were displayed or compromised in each of these situations. We can also review the following list and evaluate how much it means to us to first have these values, and then to evaluate how much discomfort we experience when those we encounter, these values being compromised, especially by those in our inner circles,.

Here is a list of some of the values we may want to use in our evaluation: honesty, loyalty, devotion, tolerance, sharing, caring, mentoring, adaptability, competitiveness, open- mindedness, curiosity, supportiveness, willingness to lead by example, decisiveness, ability to compromise, flexibility, standing by one's convictions, communicative, dependable, and tenacity along with any others that we know to be pertinent.

From our list of values, we should be able to determine which values are so dear to us and we are such staunch holders of, that we simply would not be comfortable bringing anyone who compromises these values into our inner circles.

If we encounter individuals with whom we share quite a lot in common, but who would conflict with our core values, we must consciously work to find a compromise or ensure that we avoid any situation that would cause us to have proximity to those behaviors.

In our day to day activities, we can figure out what component needs are dominant by our emotional reactions to, and the various circumstances that evoke our emotional reactions.

Here are some questions that we can ask ourselves to assist us in finding out which of our three components are dominant. This will also assist us in determining our core values: Would I be happier if I could acquire more objects I desire? Would I cut corners to gain more than someone else? How is my self- esteem related to what I own or wear, i.e. my car or my clothes? How is my self-esteem related to my knowledge? How is my self-esteem related to acceptance or rejection by others? Am I respectful of those who work for me or perform functions that society classifies as lower than mine? Are my associations based on competition or similarities? Am I apprehensive of others or situations of which I know little or nothing? Is it important to me that I associate mainly with individuals at my social, political or economic level? Am I comfortable engaging neighbors and, strangers in casual conversation?

Answers to these questions can give us much insight into the values that we have consciously or subconsciously incorporated into our beings, and which now dominate our characters. We are who we are, we also have the ability to adapt and change any personality traits that we choose.

We also have a lot in common with everyone around us based on our common physiology. Some of the superficial differences between ourselves and others are based on our possessions, our chosen career or certain abilities with which we may have been blessed. These differences do not change the fact that we are all more alike than different. When those differences are based in other artifacts outside our physical, emotional and spiritual components, when we are focused on differences with individuals based on our possessions or status, we are likely to create relationships that may be based on a never ending cycle of competition, instead of being based on what makes us more compatible.

If your happiness is primarily based on your acquisition of physical objects or association with others based on their possessions, you are dominated by your physical component. With some spiritual component development and fostering a desire to be of service to others, you can nurture many relationships that reflect some of the caring that would emanate from you, and are not simply based on competition, or worse – associating with others simply to enjoy the fruits of someone's labors.

If your sense of self-worth and happiness is tied to the acceptance and adulation of others, you are very vulnerable to manipulation and your relationships may tend to be fleeting, as circumstances often will intercede and cause the level of adulation you receive to fluctuate. As a consequence, your reactions often will be discouraging to long term relationships. If however you foster some balance, so that your passion is tempered with commitment, and you are wise in choosing those who instinctively reflect your values, your journey will be rewarding and pleasurable.

Even if you are dominated by your spiritual component and your values are rooted in respect and caring, you must develop your emotional and physical component so that you achieve the balance to properly relate to others, and thus be able to enjoy meaningful harmonious relationships.

Happiness is a personal emotion we must learn to prolong. Like all emotions, happiness is internal to each of us and can be influenced by us. By taking the time to find our core values, we can then set out to create our circles of individuals whose interactions contribute to our happiness. To truly prolong our feeling of happiness, our inner circle must be based in spiritual bonding. We must select individuals with whom we are not obsessed in being in a constant state of competition, and our inner circles must be about caring and sharing the adventures of this journey. Those we select for these positions should undergo a careful screening of their values to ensure that they have demonstrated the ability to care for another as we would care for them. We must also share trust and respect. It should now be apparent that although physical possessions are not a deterrent for inner circle relationships, neither are they a requirement.

Reciprocity in caring, sharing, trust and respect are paramount for all inner circle relationships. The degree to which these values are part of our core values will determine how likely and how strongly we bond with others.

Realizing that our values influence the types and quality of relationships we share, we should be committed to periodically reviewing our behaviors to determine if we have indeed made a complete list of our core values. If we determine that there are values we admire and would like to incorporate into ourselves, we must be aware that we are in fact making changes to our character, and so these changes should never be undertaken lightly.

Understanding ourselves, attempting to gain mastery of our emotions, and cultivating the ability to influence the type and quality of our relationships, is dependent on us constantly being aware of these core values. Since most of the exercises presented here are ongoing for the duration of our journeys, we all have less time to be bored! The reward, however, is a constantly expanding pathway filled with positive experiences.

The five step program

The following are the five steps we must learn and we will reference in order to effectively perform any task we may encounter. These steps are the basis of all self-improvement and will be referenced in whole or in part in all exercises. Take some time to study and even memorize these steps. Whenever and wherever possible, consciously incorporate them into your daily activities.

1. Breathe

2. Relax

3. Focus

4. Set a task

5. Close the gap

Breathe

Many volumes have been written on and about breathing and breath control. You can reference any of these materials for details and background information on other breathing techniques and their benefits. The breath is obviously essential to life. However, even a casual look around us, will inform us that most individuals we encounter are very shallow breathers. If you make a sincere attempt at performing these exercises, you will in fact learn to increase your air intake. and use more of your lungs for better aeration of your blood and vital organs. You will also learn how to breathe using your lower lung and how to control your diaphragm. The focus here is on performance, not technical details, results are what matters.

For most of us, our emotional states influence our breathing, this happens unconsciously. What we will now be doing will be to take control of our breathing to influence our physical and emotional state.

There are two aspects of breathing on which we will need to focus, both will be addressed by the exercises. We will learn to take in more air and also to control how we take in that air, focusing on performing the exercise correctly will allow us to realize the benefits, regardless of if or how those benefits are enumerated.

Preferably in a lying position, although standing or sitting works, place one or both hands on your stomach, breathe in slowly but very deeply. Each breath should be silent and just inhaling should take about five to eight seconds. As you inhale, you should feel your stomach rising slowly. Hold this breath for two to three seconds, then slowly exhale. Exhaling should take about three to five seconds. Let your body decide how much rest if any, you take before inhaling again.

Focus on this breathing pattern, and try to complete several full breaths by repeating the above steps. You should be feeling very relaxed, as you would have shut out much of the noise that distracts, and your body will be thankful for the aeration!

Although this step may seem pretty simple, like so many processes that are automated in our bodies, it is the most important step. Take the time to learn this step and try to incorporate it into you daily activities. Whenever you feel uncomfortable due to external stresses, or even if your internal processes, such as thoughts or pain, are causing you distress, try to take at least three deep breaths using the above procedure.

In time, you should be able to consciously perform this exercise, even when walking or jogging, to "calm your nerves". When you are challenged with interpersonal relationship issues, you should be able to perform these exercises without anyone noticing. With practice you will learn to induce the calm that makes you comfortable within a few breaths, which should take less than a minute, and you'll be able to execute all your plans more effectively.

Relax

The above step should have started the relaxation phase. This relaxation is not only for sleeping, but it is geared more towards clearing out emotional debris and quieting the physical, so that we can get on to the next step. While we relax, we should focus only on our breathing, and not on anything that could be a distractionThis is your time for yourself, and the results you feel will be determined by your efforts to master these techniques. If we need to rest, the process of breathing and relaxation while clearing our thoughts can also be conducive to a restful sleep, it can eliminate the need for chemical sleep aids.

If you had difficulty sleeping, it can be helpful you to incorporate the following exercise. Picture yourself alone in some place in nature that you enjoy. A beach, a meadow, a desert, or wherever else you like. The purpose is for you to choose a place where you feel very comfortable, so you can relax in this place. Set yourself a goal of walking to some destination. As you walk towards this destination, enjoy all the details of your surroundings. Focus on details, but let everything go by, as you are on your way to your destination. Be there, focus on the details of enjoying your stay in this place, and exclude everyone and everything from intruding on your enjoyment of this journey. How does the wind feel? Isn't it wonderful to be able to enjoy this peaceful place? Enjoy the colors, enjoy the sounds, enjoy nature.

Focus

Once you have stabilized your breathing and you are feeling relaxed, you can now set your focus on one task to the exclusion of almost everything else. In order to do this, it is important that you do not try to hurry yourself, as the ability to snap into this deep concentration mode may take varying amounts of time but you will master this in time. It may help to close your eyes, or to fix your eyes on something in the vicinity. The purpose is to lock out things that are in your vicinity, and to focus on the details of your mental process. Even if your eyes are open, you should not be focused on the details of anything in front of you, so in fact you should be looking but not seeing. You are now developing the ability to concentrate on and seek solutions to whatever issues you may encounter. As you become better at this exercise, you may eventually be able to become a conduit for solutions that you currently cannot imagine! If you do, you would have tapped into the universal source of knowledge.

For the present, practice to focus on one thought or process, with your eyes closed or looking without seeing for fifteen, then thirty seconds until you can lose yourself in this mode of concentration for three to five minutes at a minimum.

As you repeat this exercise, over time you will develop or sharpen your ability to process facts related to any problem, and thus come up with poignant solutions in relatively short periods of time.

Set a task

Setting tasks is something that we all are very good at, however now that we have focused on one activity, we can drill down to the details of what is required to complete that task. This is our planning phase for upcoming activities, the more detailed our plans, the more likely we are to manage a successful implementation. The name of this exercise is somewhat of a misnomer because in this exercise we will in fact be dealing with multiple tasks, we are creating our plans.

At this point, you need to be aware of the level of detail that must be incorporated into your planning. Be aware that you can take different aerial views for your plan. Consider the following scenario as an example. If you were to take a ten thousand foot view of land where you were planning a city, you would plan the layout of streets and the location of buildings etc. It is only when you take a much closer view, let's say at street level, that you would be concerned with the details of the materials to be used in construction. Therefore, do not mix or confuse the perspective in your planning, do not concern yourself with details if you are creating very high level plans, but be aware that these details will have to be resolved during a subsequent review. Make notes of any areas that cause discomfort because there are unknowns or there are dependencies on factors over which you have no control.

Be aware that trying to implement a plan that was created with a ten thousand foot view of things may be worse than implementing without planning. This is because you may be filled with unjustified expectations, and thus endure a lot of disappointments. It would be similar to us planning a dinner but not taking the time to account for the space requirements, the availability of the ingredients for our dishes, ensuring that all those individuals we need involved are available or the time needed to procure or prepare those dishes.

So, we must be aware of our level of planning, and when we perform our detailed plans, we must include accommodations for time and expense where appropriate.

For example, if we have decided to research certain foods, this step is where we will decide where, when and how we will perform this research, if the task(s) involves the use of tools or at some point we will be dependent on the actions of others. This step is where we will make a note of what is required, so that we can gather tools or make necessary contacts, this is a preparedness phase for the task, so that we are properly prepared to execute in the next phase.

Close the gap

This is the action phase, this is where we execute our plans, or perform those actions to implement our strategies. This is the phase where we achieve our goals. We have performed the preliminary and preparatory work, we have created plans that are clearly defined, we have performed whatever tasks are preliminary, and now we must 'close the gap' that exists between planning and execution to bring the fruits of our planning to reality. All our preparations mean nothing, if we do not execute at this stage. Results are achieved during this phase, and without this step, our accomplishments are minimal if any. It is vitally important that when you perform any review of your actions, that your time and energy is spent reviewing this step to determine your accomplishments.

Developing "The Vision Thing"

Vision gives purpose to our actions. In order to be our most productive, not only do we need a strong will, but we must have a heightened sense of vision. Not because everything we envision will turn out exactly the way we plan or wish, but because vision serves to provide a point of focus for our actions, regardless of the circumstances in which we find ourselves. We can only consciously serve a meaningful purpose when we have developed our vision. If we have not developed it, our actions can best be targeted to serve in pursuing the vision of another. The following exercise can serve to assist in developing this critical attribute. However, we must recognize that when we seek to develop internal abilities, similar to physical exercise, we can have a coach, but the benefits we realize are dependent on the amount of work we put into achieving our personal goals.

Without vision it is difficult to establish goals, and thus work becomes mostly aimless. The more clearly defined our visions of what we need to accomplish, the more focused our actions, and so it will be less likely that we are distracted from achieving our goals.

Although this ability can be used for all the following, this exercise is not about achieving the goals as defined by the vision of anyone else, or clearly stating a problem so that someone else can define a comprehensive solution, or for defining tasks that need to be completed to achieve some end.

Again, this is about you. These exercises are meant primarily for you to learn how to obtain a very clear vision of your objectives and to enable you to create a very detailed enumeration of the tasks required to achieve that goal. Vision contains some aspects of spatial reasoning and your abilities in this area should also be enhanced.

Following are a couple redundant reminders before we delve into this exercise. This is not about how, why or where as relates to anyone else, so please, focus only on yourself. Also, although we may be able to rewrite history and paint any picture of the future, none of us can change the past, the past is what it is, it is a path we have travelled but, it does not own our today. The exercises we will be performing are in the present and the past has no control, except for any influence we allow it over our present. Like our abilities with those around us, the past may influence our present, but it has no control over it. So please, be honest with yourself about your past, there is no need to discuss anything with anyone as you revisit your past, as this is a private journey. Furthermore, and this is extremely important, *do not focus on the actions of anyone else who you may have encountered in the past.* Today you cannot change their motivations or actions, and this exercise can actually be counterproductive if all the focus is not only on yourself and your thoughts, motivation and actions. No benefit will accrue to you if you attempt to focus on the actions of others, and consequently no time or energy should be expended in this area. You cannot change the actions of anyone in the past, even your own. The objective here is to revisit the path of your past journey, and review your actions to take positive lessons from reviewing your past and to learn how you could have made better decisions in the past for future reference.

Our lives are journeys through time, your past is the road you have traveled. To best navigate the road ahead, we must learn to first control ourselves, so that our actions are considered and deliberate, regardless of the circumstances in which we find ourselves. There is no magic here, we need to do the work to build the abilities we need to be successful. What you must be aware of in performing this exercise is that you are building your own personal cache of goodies, or bag of tricks from which you can draw whenever you want. Ok, let's start!

From the five step program, breathe (at least three deep breaths), relax, focus.

Now go back in your life to the earliest time that you can clearly remember, not some time when things were fuzzy, but go to those experiences that are very clear in you memory. Walk forward over all the items that you think were significant, do not hesitate to move on - this is an exercise that should take minutes not years! In every significant interaction with others remember, you cannot change anything now, the objective is to review your preparations and actions. Was there any knowledge or forethought that you utilized to influence those past actions and the related results? Make notes if necessary. What knowledge could have assisted you to obtain a more beneficial outcome? If the results of any reviewed interactions were particularly positive, was it just incidental or were there some preparation of actions on your behalf that contributed to the outcome?

Unless most of the significant events in your past were purely unexpected acts of nature, you must take responsibility for your contributions. Be gentle with yourself, when you have made mistakes in the past, do not blame anyone, this is about you and how you can improve your future. Blame does nothing to help you in the future, do not put excuses into your bag of tricks if you want a richer future.

This is why this exercise is private, you get to honestly review yourself, and if there were mistakes in the past, make preparations to improve your reaction if a similar event is encountered in the future. Where your performance was exemplary in the past and with the benefit of experiences since that time, ask yourself: could you do better now?. Become aware of your preparations, your actions, the manner in which you executed those triumphs, make notes and add any refinements, so that you can be even better the next time you apply those techniques. Regardless of whether the events you review are physical accomplishments, events that had an emotional impact, or actions that gave you personal satisfaction, take the good from each and put them into your store for the future.

Continue this review until you've come to the present. Be true to yourself, review your actions without excuses or commentary, these are past events - do not judge. It is ok to take several sessions to complete this exercise as time permits. Once again, this is personal, private and should be totally focused on you.

As you approach the current date and time, review events more closely. How do you react to events around you? The answer to this question will reveal what components are dominant in your being in case ther are any confusions. Are your emotions, such as joy, sorrow, anger, bitterness etc, based on receiving or losing physical things or on the actions of others? Again do not concentrate on others, this is about you! As you stand today, what would make you most happy? What would make you sad? What would you most like to gain? Lose?

Vision is mostly passive as you are simply performing observations. This is where you get to step four in the five step program, set a task. Your review so far should lead to planning. Based on your review of your journey up to this point, think about those significant events. Did you react in a manner that was appropriate to obtain the result you wanted? What prior events prepared you to make the decisions or take the actions you did? Are there any individuals who provided you with knowledge or other assistance to assist with your preparations? Are there any individuals with qualities that you admired or emulated to assist you with your decisions or actions? Are you better prepared today? What could you have done better if presented with similar circumstances today? What attributes of your character were the most disturbing or likely to cause you, or those you care about, problems? What attributes led to pleasant outcomes? How do your strengths and weaknesses relate now to "back then"?

At the end of this and every vision development session, you should have a sense of accomplishment and wellbeing due to you adding to yourself, and your cache, as you continue consciously preparing for your tomorrows. Out of every negative you will take responsibility, but do not take negative baggage forward. You will find something positive, in some cases just surviving is a positive, so that you are better prepared to at least eliminate past mistakes and you are more likely able to positively influence everything from casual encounters to deep personal relationships. This should also enable you to be better prepared to achieve whatever goals you set for yourself.

After you have completed the review of your past, you may also choose to do some review of those you admire. Use the experience of mentors to also add to your cache, so that your repertoire for dealing with events in the future is even more enhanced.

Resolve to smile more often. Resolve to strengthen and influence others to bring out the best in all you encounter, and you be like a light to all. Be real, there is beauty in everyone. Challenge yourself to find that beauty, so that you attain some degree of mastery in finding common ground with others you encounter, and every day will be more rewarding. As you continue working towards this end, your relationships will become deeper, and you will find more individuals you can consciously include in your inner circles. You will also be able to have positive experiences with even those who you must relegate to distant outer circles.

Strengthening your Willpower

The first and most important requirement for building or strengthening our willpower is an earnest desire to achieve some goals. Next, we must recognize that a stronger will or more willpower would be beneficial in achieving those goals. Without a desire to have a strong willpower, no amount of talking, reading or anything else will be of material use to us. Just as we can visibly observe those who refuse to perform physical exercises to strengthen their physical components, we can also observe those who, within a short time span become desirous of constantly seeking external support instead of having the desire to increase their true inner strength. If we are not honest with ourselves, we can literally make hundreds of excuses for not reaching our objectives, achieving our goals, or accomplishing those tasks that are required of us, due to our lack of will power.

Once again this process is about you, not anyone you know or have known. It is about you focusing on self improvement through increasing your inner strength, so that you can transform your life by being able to accomplish those goals that you set yourself. If you truly have the desire and will commit to these exercises, very shortly, you, as well as others will see the results of your work. Just as we can be coached in a routine of physical exercises, we can be coached with our will, and those who persevere and are dedicated to a course of action will reap the benefits. Those benefits will be commensurate with your innate ability, and the amount of time and effort you devote to your self- improvement.

By strengthening your willpower, you will be able to focus more intently on planning, as well as execution of those plans. With your enhanced willpower all your results will be more rewarding, because of your increased dedication and correspondingly higher achievements.

You will increase your willpower by performing some of the same exercises detailed in the five step program. You must control your breathing, so you can relax and focus on the task to be performed. Keep in mind the analogy of training to increase your physical strength: you would start with manageable weights (imagine a comfortable weight to perform curls for your biceps), and over time gradually increase those weights to place more stress on the muscles, the muscles, in turn respond by getting stronger. Similarly, start with simple tasks and with time slowly increase the complexity and/or effort required to complete each new project.

Attention to detail is important here. The first few instances that you perform these exercises, take whatever time is necessary to ensure that you have taken control of your breathing, and ensure your focus is solely on planning the task(s) you intend to perform. Then make certain that you complete the task to your satisfaction without allowing yourself to be distracted without good reason or excuses. If you find that you are distracted you may need to choose another time or place to perform these exercises. Again, at the end of every successful session, you should be feeling a wonderful calm, and yet somewhat exhilarating sense of accomplishment based on some of the side effects of these exercises. In time and with repetition, much of this training should become a part of your subconscious, so you will perform them without having to consciously think about the various steps.

Following are some suggestions for tasks. There must be things that you need to accomplish, but have been putting off because they are not your favorite ways to spend your time, or you could resolve to research some information on the internet in order to perform some subsequent action, i.e. look- up a recipe and prepare a meal, start a small home improvement project, clean out the refrigerator, perform breathing exercises, reconcile a budget, perform some needed repairs, take a vehicle for service etc.. What is important is that you consciously decide that you will perform these actions. Before starting any physical action., decide exactly what you will be doing. Plans change but try to get in the habit of getting an idea of how much time and effort is required before you start performing work. If for example, you decided to clean out the refrigerator, decide before you start on how much time you are going to spend and create tasks that fit within that timeframe. Be flexible, but be in control of the scope of the tasks that you decide to perform.

Passion is to life what flavor is to food. We should not strive to eliminate passion, just be in control of your own. Control of your emotions is an exercise that is especially rewarding as you can project the image of yourself you feel is most representative of who you are. Emotional control is also an area in which we are constantly in need of practice, since everywhere we go, everyone we meet, there will be opportunityiesto practice control of your emotions. Be real, don' be stiff, no one wants to deal with stiff, mechanical, or people who fake emotions.

There will be many 'bumps' in the road during your journey through time, react with passion when needed, just use every opportunity to be in control of that passion, you may be able to prolong many pleasurable activities because of your self-control.

Imagine for a moment that you want to obtain some certification, which is required so you can pursue one of your life's passions. If you had access to some of the best tutors, all the most relevant texts and materials and also had the time, there would still be no guarantee that you would accomplish that goal if you did not have the willpower to focus and dedicate yourself to doing the necessary work As another example, if you planned on upgrading your garage and you had all the materials and tools - because you took the time to plan, unless you had the willpower to get out and start that task, it would never get completed.

As you repeat these willpower exercises, think of yourself preparing for then going on a journey. The more prepared you are, the more likely you will pass your milestones and reach your destination in the expected time. From every setback or failure, review quickly, be determined, find a path around or through if necessary, but learn from the setback. Some of our best lessons come from these challenges.

You need to start with small tasks so that you have success, because constant failure... well it takes more inner strength to overcome multiple setbacks, so just as you would not go to a gym and attempt to use the maximum weight..., be gentle with yourself, allow yourself room to grow into handling more prodigious events. Smile, have a positive attitude when there are unexpected challenges or setbacks, let you inner strength provide a lead to your physical demeanor. You will become adept at controlling your emotions and nurturing in that relaxed yet not complacent attitude that will indicate your confidence in your abilities. You will become better at handling the stresses that are a part of modern living, you will have a more positive outlook, even in the face of what many may consider failure, because you will be too busy learning from the current setback and preparing to overcome anything similar in the future. You will become more adaptable, which is key to not only surviving, but thriving as the environment changes.

Issues..., Personal Issues!

We are complex beings, each unique, our satisfaction and achievement of happiness is tied to meeting our component needs, which are normally represented as the realization of our personal goals. Our personal goals are linked to our internal makeup (nature), responses to external factors that may have been part of our upbringing (nurture), as well as influences by the societies in which we are immersed (culture).

By nature we are composed of three components, who we are, and how we interact with everyone and everything around us is partly a result of our responses to the needs of these components. As I have detailed in "Spiritual Renewal - renewing our pact", our three components are the physical, emotional and spiritual. Each of these components is a part of our individual makeup, and our character is determined by the interactions between these components, and our assertion of control over the needs of each.

Our lives are journeys through time, each of us has our own unique experiences even though we may take the road most traveled for our culture and seem to all be on the same path, even in the same place and time.

For each of us, each day of our life is like a cup that must be filled with personal experiences, whether that be sitting around, enhancing our knowledge, with happiness or with sadness. Tomorrow we get a new cup that must be filled again.

With self-control, we take responsibility for the contents and the manner in which they are mixed, even when we have no control of the ingredients poured into our cup, we take responsibility for the way we react to the events that unfold as our personal experiences. By controlling our reaction to circumstances, we are in fact laying the groundwork for subsequent events and seeking to ensure positive outcomes in our future, instead of allowing these events to become unpleasant baggage which we inadvertently take with us to poison, detract from, or cause decay in our future experiences. If we are thankful to be able to have a new cup every day, we would try to put something positive into every day, and thus build a positive base for our future.

All our 'issues' are based in conflicts, which are stresses caused by our needs being unmet, or conflicts between what we encounter and our expectations. These conflicts may be internal or external.

Most of us are problem solvers, unfortunately most often for other people! We have solutions to fit any problem that just about anyone else may have, we just have a little trouble resolving our issues with our solutions! This book is about empowering us to seek to strengthen ourselves first, so that we become the examples of solutions instead of being hypocritical proposers of solutions that we are unwilling or unable to implement in our own lives.

Here again we may benefit from the skills of trained mentors, but we must at all times be conscious of our responsibilities and actions in obtaining solutions to our issues. There may be situations where our actions may seem to be limited to showing up for an appointment but this is never the case, we always have a responsibility to prepare ourselves physically, emotionally and spiritually to assist any professional who may be involved in assisting us with a solution to our problems.

Ideally, we all have extended families, with whom we have strong bonds established over many years of harmony and some conflict, and whom we can always turn to in times of doubt or crisis for both strength and advice. We should however always seek to nurture a network of individuals we admire for the work they have done, in areas where we may need assistance. Just as important as finding credible mentors based on their experiences, is that we must recognize those who have disqualified themselves from being credible mentors through our use of the "village view" principle. It should not have to be stated here, but due to the prevalence of this type of behavior, it is something we must not forget.

For example, it makes no sense to be taking weight loss and dieting advice from anyone who needs to be on a diet. If anyone were to inform us of the value of a certain diet, based on the "village view" principle we must ask ourselves: why aren't they beneficiaries of it? and why are they unable to maintain a set weight before they start extolling it's virtues? It may be fine to hear of the shortcuts they have taken, but in some regards they are actually discrediting the product by being a spokesperson for something that it would appear does not work.

It makes no sense to take advice on forming or maintaining a treasured relationship from anyone who by their life experiences would appear to not treasure long-term relationships! Please, do not take advice on how issues in your relationships should be handled from those who have a history of troubled relationships or even worse are participants in the "shoplifting" principle. Following their advice is a sure way to introduce the same or similar issues into your life – in which case you would now really need their advice!

When we seek solutions to issues, we should seek out those individuals that do not create other issues of a similar magnitude, or solutions that are temporary and may cause more harm in the long-term. Problem resolution requires that we have some vision to ensure that the path chosen does not lead to more complications in the future. Vision is also required to ensure that we have some semblance of predictability in our journeys. We each also need a strong will to be a source of the determination required to 'close the gap' between the talk and action, planning, and execution so that we can take the required actions, in an attempt to influence the quality of the encounters that affect our experiences in the future.

Even if individuals, who do not have the willpower or self-control to implement a workable solution, were to propose this solution to us, and we were able to successfully implement 'their' solution, with our self-control and willpower, we would more than likely lose a friend!

By way of example, let's take on a couple of issues that you or those in your circle (more on this later) may be dealing with now or in the future: weight control, drug addiction, parent/child relationships, and peer/mate personal relationships. Please be aware that the focus of this information is to empower you, to give you the tools to make you stronger and better at making those decisions, and performing those actions which positively affect you and those in your circle.

Therefore, *the focus will always be on what you can do and how you can accomplish these goals*. In order to stand upright without support, or to assist in supporting others, we must at the very least, have a strong spine. Thus, if you must learn to and perform actions that make you stronger so you can stand unassisted by others, you will be more valuable to both yourself and to those who may need to lean on you from time to time.

You must gain internal strength to stand alone. To accomplish this, you must first want to stand, you must have a strong will to persevere and learn from your mistakes in order to grow to the point where you can walk along with those who are each on their individual journeys, maybe towards a common or similar destination.

Let's take a look at some of the issues that we or some of our loved ones have to deal with and what actions will result in positive outcomes:

Weight control

Some of life's basic pleasures leave no visible signs of our participation, however, eating is not one of them. Although we can attribute our extra weight to any number of causes, this much is inescapable: if we stop eating, eventually we lose weight.

To attain lasting success, we must use both our vision and willpower. First take a look back. We must have the ability to recognize (vision) the path traveled, which resulted in us being where we are currently. If we can honestly review our actions (not motivation or reasons why) over the period during which we gained weight, we should be able to identify the actions we took that resulted in our current status, regardless of the reasons. Next we must look ahead to where we want to be in the future. Based on your individual ability, select a timeframe, set some milestones for yourself. Be kind to yourself; be realistic and recognize the time it took to get to this point, and thus expect to first build you willpower before, and as you struggle to achieve both your short and long-term goals (milestones/destination).

The further you have descended into a valley, the more time and effort (willpower) will be needed to ascend to the heights you would like to attain. This is your journey, you are the primary beneficiary of your actions. Recognize that diets are like shortcuts that may be rife with perils, but even if they are not, the actions that you must now incorporate into your daily life would not be the same actions involved during a shortcut. It is the difference in discipline and actions required between losing and maintaining weight.

Now that you have set yourself some tasks, which may include the research to find the tools that would assist you in achieving your milestones If you had maintained your weight in a range that you felt comfortable, then, due to some set of circumstances, some of your actions caused the additional weight gain, you now have a reference point on what your diet should be like, once you have completed your weight loss. If however you do not have such a reference point, you will need to research, implement and periodically review a new diet.

What is important here is that we must recognize that in order to maintain our weight, we must find a balance between our level of activity and the amount of food we ingest. Often what is needed is a lifestyle change. These are the changes that you make in the way you travel on this journey. In order for positive results to be a part of your journey from this day onward, you must find a way to incorporate these behaviors into your day to day activities. If you don't, you know that it will not be long before you need another shortcut. Be true to yourself.

What is required for us to "close the gap" between planning and executing our plan is to spend time increasing your willpower, assuming you've done whatever research is necessary to get the information needed to make these far-reaching decisions. Increasing our willpower is analogous to going to the gym to develop those muscles that you will need to perform a physical task. You may need to re-read, become very familiar with, and perform the exercises in the chapter "The five step program". You may also want to enroll in some of our courses for the equivalence of having a personal trainer, in order to better prepare you for the heavy lifting ahead.

It cannot hurt if you have others of a like mind, who have developed their vision and self-control to assist you while you are not quite strong enough. You are fortunate if there are individuals in your personal circle to assist and be your cheering section (emotional boosters), until you are strong enough to not require it. Watch your relationships grow as you grow stronger!

Create positive diversions in your life. These serve to fill your cup every day, just like your personal circle of people who act as confidants and source of strength as well as provide reality checks, your diversions should be few in number and sufficiently intense to hold your attention so that you can immerse yourself to the exclusion of distractions. Be passionate about these diversions, just be passionate period!

Drug addiction

In most cases, drugs are used to either stimulate or dull certain emotional or physical reactions to factors that we feel we cannot influence. If these are a result of unmet needs, we may need to find other external stimulation to replace those that were formerly supplied by chemicals. Besides the effect of vision and willpower on our self-esteem, both, our ability to manage our physical and emotional needs, as well as the ability to consciously cultivate a circle of individuals with whom we can share activities that can serve as a diversion from those things we seek to avoid, will be enhanced. We can then fill our cups with activities, including introspection, which are fulfilling and do not require the use of chemical stimulants. As we cultivate closer personal circles, we will also be able to on a more regular basis partake in activities with other individuals with whom we share similar values and interests. This will reduce or eliminate any depression or negative feelings which we currently manage by the use of drugs. Positive relationships should also lead to healthy eating habits and should help to incorporate exercises to bring out the best health possible for all members of the group, and thus satisfy most of the unmet needs that result in drug addiction.

Parent/Child personal relationships

Children need mentors, guides and teacher. If parents serve in this role, they will always be admired and looked up to by their children. Issues are normally created by the actions of those parents, who abscond from this very important role and in many instances try to be a peer to their own children while forsaking their primary duties!

The type and amount of work needed to correct any issues in parent/children relationships depend on the age of the children. For children below or within the three to eleven ("the 3211") age group, most of the changes must be made by the parents. These parents will have to learn to become effective guides and teachers. This can be accomplished only if these parents have the desire and willpower to perform these duties. They can also use relationship mentors to learn the habits and techniques needed to transform first themselves, then their children into the compatible parts of successful relationships.

Here is the one trait that parents must be aware of if they are to be successful, this trait is a part of any good relationship. This must be apparent in the relationship of any whom we choose are relationship mentors, it is respect.

Respect is the last thing that is lost in a good relationship. Parents need to cultivate respect, both by their actions in being respectable and by deterring any disrespect from their children at a very early age. If this is not accomplished, it is highly improbable that any good relationship can be established. It must be noted here that any incidents of discipline or curtailment of privileges should be a miniscule percentage of the time spent interacting with children. Any negative experiences as a result of this teaching of disciple should be overwhelmed by positive experiences, not as compensation for those incidents – in fact we may want those incident to be remembered- but to fill most of the time spent developing or maintaining the relationship with positive memories.

Consider the following analogy: as a guide and teacher we lead our children on this pathway, we should seek to make that pathway as wide as possible so that all have quite a bit of leeway in their thoughts, actions and choices, so that individual growth is encouraged. However, the lines that we set to delineate the edges of this pathway should be very clear and the consequences spelt out very clearly. We can also teach forgiveness and mercy by the way we enforce the consequences as in the number of "chances" anyone is given before we really resort to punishment. This can also serve to build our children sense of empowerment, because they are allowed to make the choices to continually be in our good graces, as opposed to dealing with us when they have broken clearly defined rules.

This may seem too harsh for many parents and many who are not parents. Parents however should be tasked to raise their children, and in order to be effective, we must develop the ability to take a "village view" of those who give advice. In other words, we give priority to the advice from those who are qualified by experience we can admire as we apply our own knowledge and try to improve our own lives and the lives of our offspring.

In cases of conflict involving parents and children who have already passed the "3211" stage, but are not yet adults, it is more important for the parents to seek to understand the base of the culture, which has been assimilated by these young adults, in order to influence them and have a positive relationship. As with all things including relationships, we must understand the value of time. We must also remember that we can influence and teach more by being agreeable than by focusing on conflict. And when we must agree to disagree, we do it in a way that does not result in a loss of respect, as this will lead to the demise of any good relationship.

If we understand that most issues are a result of unmet needs or conflicts with the need of internal components, we, as parents, must learn to objectively seek to understand the need that is not being met or the conflict that is causing the turmoil or disharmony. Is it physical, emotional or spiritual? In order to be successful, we must be able to make this determination with none or very little of our projecting ourselves and our values and associated baggage into the role of the child. Once we can confirm with the child that we have an understanding of the "issue(s)", we can then subtly seek to influence, by providing guidance or serving that need, in a manner that provides a positive outcome and draws from our knowledge and experiences.

Peer/Mate personal relationships

With all peer relationships, we must recognize that our interactions with others are like circles that overlap, there will always be areas that do not fit exactly. As the enlightened, we need to recognize that those areas of overlap are where we experience harmony with others. We must then seek to set ground rules when necessary for those interactions that involve our differences or those parts of our circles that do not overlap. Oftentimes it is best to simply see these areas as 'our thing' and 'their thing'. Key to maintaining a positive relationship is to respect those differences. We may often need to compromise if our differences have a direct bearing on our relationship. Consider the following example: if an associate consumes alcohol and we do not, and we are offended by the smell of alcohol, in order to have interaction without conflict, we should let our associate know that, while we do not intend to disrespectful or require that they curtail that activity, we would be appreciative, if they would do something to mask the smell, as we are not comfortable with it during our interaction with them.

As with all personal communications, we must use our self-control to appear upbeat and positive, rather than accusatory or demeaning. If we are able to laugh at our weaknesses, and cultivate our awareness of other peoples' reactions to us, we will be able to influence even those who may appear different from ourselves. This is an ability we learn from being conscious of the values of others around us, based on observing their emotional reactions to circumstances. With a little practice, we will soon be able to find those common items that form the basis of a mutually beneficial interaction, if not the basis of a good relationship.

With all interactions, we must weigh the self-esteem of individuals, even those who may not be very communicative, we must learn to make an assessment of what they think of themselves, so that we can more suitably position our mode of communicating, to be best received by each individual.

For the journey ahead…

The knowledge and exercises presented here provide the basis of an ongoing and continual growth and learning process. As we lessen our conceit of the unknown or unexplained, we should constantly seek to be growing and accumulating both knowledge and experiences that enrich and reward.

Much of our current state of existence is tied to our health. Our science has revealed quite a lot about the connection between the foods we consume and the state of our health. It is reasonable to assume that there is still quite a lot to learn, however, the conceit that invades the egos of many of our scientists would have you believe that indeed, everything that needs to be known, already has been learnt.

This process is about you and your personal growth, ask yourself 'how many times have we been proven wrong when we choose to eat processed products instead of eating natural foods?'. Think of your diet in terms of prevention as well as healing, research and share information, but do not be misguided by fads and 'miracle' or 'wonder' foods without some demonstrable proof. Expand your diet, get nutrients from as many different sources as you can afford, your health is one of your most precious possessions. Even without regular strenuous exercise, a diverse and well thought out diet can ensure you of good health. Without scientific proof, I would estimate that more than seventy percent of your health, or the lack thereof, can be traced back to your diet.

Fad "diets" are like shortcuts, they can get you from point A to B because you are unhappy with being at point A. We must be hopeful that there are no serious negative consequences associated with taking this shortcut, but then the normal journey continues. If the behaviors and ingredients do not become an integral part of the journey, it is just a matter of time before another shortcut is needed.

What is really needed in almost all cases are lifestyle changes, not just shortcuts akin to being on vacation from your regular lifestyle. Without lifestyle changes, diets will become a recurring theme, which is fine for those who desire some conversation topics, but not if you truly desire to retain control of one of your most precious possessions.

As we enhance our vision and build our willpower, we must also build awareness of ourselves and be conscious of our actions and reactions to those around us. Even when through our knowledge and experience, we are certain that we are correct in our viewpoints, we must be cognizant of how we communicate, so that we can be most effective.

We must learn through self-control to be tactful, as well as to be able to recognize when our point of view is so different that our audience is unreceptive, based on deep seated issues that may not be directly related to our topic. We must recognize that we cannot change anyone. We can present information that at some time becomes relevant and influences changes in people and systems, and so it is important that we strive to find common ground, if just so that our message is heard. Recognize, we cannot change anyone and we may not be able to directly make a change, but we can influence change whenever it happens. Awareness of ourselves must afford us the opportunity to see ourselves in the bigger picture; we must recognize that we are part of a larger community, a community on which we depend and which also depends on us.

As part of our awareness of ourselves and our relationships to the larger community, we should take the time to investigate how our emotional, physical and spiritual needs are met by our interactions with other members of our community. This should lead us to take a more active role in establishing and nurturing those relationships that support our development and achieve our goals, including our spiritual need for service/sacrifice.

Each of us is born with certain abilities which, in combination with our character, make us unique. These special abilities are our God given talents, and if we are lucky (luck is when preparedness meets opportunity!) we will be able to perform some function in the society that makes use of that talent. The most fortunate are those who are paid for their services to the community, they are doubly rewarded! If we are to be among the fortunate in a society where our jobs are themselves a reward, we must understand the concept of talent and effort.

On our journey through time, we all strive to fill every day with some enjoyment. Since every day is like a cup that must be filled, we must try to control some of the ingredients that are placed in our cup, as well as how we mix those ingredients when we have little or no control over their placement in our cup. By putting concerted efforts into developing our talents, we will find that by being influential in the environment in which we are placed daily, as well as the activities in which we are involved, we have established some control over what is poured into our cup, regardless of status the society may attach to our endeavors. Work becomes almost a hobby, and we realize the benefits of being viewed as naturally good at what we do, because we thoroughly enjoy our vocation. If we have placed so much effort into developing our talents that our community rewards us sufficiently so that we are able to choose how we spend our time, we would continue to perform our function. We would do this because our work would be fulfilling to us, regardless of any associated rewards. As such, ***if <u>we</u> put adequate effort into developing our talents, our talents can be the <u>source of fulfillment of our physical, emotional and spiritual needs.</u>***

What we do each day when we interact with others is to represent ourselves. If we possess abilities that are beneficial to others, they may employ us to assist with their endeavors. Although we may be appointed to serve in some capacity, we must not be changed, we must serve to the best of our abilities, but we will not appear to become something or someone else if we stay true to ourselves. We must recognize that the value others may place on us is based on our ability, therefore by enhancing our abilities through effort, we in fact become more valuable and beneficial to others around us.

With our enhanced awareness and self- control, we will be able to be more influential in every interaction that involves individuals. We accomplish this by using our self-control to put us in the right frame of mind, as well as make whatever physical maneuvers necessary to assure positive outcomes.

We must learn to laugh at ourselves when we make mistakes, we must take responsibility for our actions, and we must be more willing to strengthen those around us, because we understand the benefits of being part of a 'strong' circle. As we learn and grow, we must recognize and be able to introduce those attributes that benefit ourselves and others. Levity is a good example: most individuals perform better when relaxed, if we can make another person smile or laugh, we influence their relaxation and often get a better response. Attempt to recognize the unique talents of others.

As we go forward in our various journeys, it will benefit us to remember at all times that almost everything we do will involve relationships, and that all relationships are personal. Whether for business or pleasure, when we interact with others, we should strive to see individuals, with their strengths and weaknesses so that we can create personal bonds whenever possible. In all interactions relating to our close inner circles, we must consider the following question, which comes from an old Chinese saying, "do you want to win, or do you want to be happy?". Learning to compromise for the greater good of stronger, inner circle relationships should be one of our goals.

We should seek mentors. Mentors are those whose life experiences we admire. Use the "village view" principle to cultivate a network of individuals who we can turn to for advice in any area of our lives. This is not as difficult as it may seem. We could approach anyone whom we admire for their ability to perform, not just words but actions as demonstrated in their life's work. We could let them know that we admire their accomplishments, and that we would like to know if they would take the time to help us, if we were in a specific situation where we believed their expertise in dealing with their own life experiences could be invaluable to us. While there are no real substitutes for experience, others have travelled the path which we now traverse. If we admire how they have conducted themselves, we should congratulate and seek to learn from them, so that we can avoid any pitfalls that may lie ahead. Using the above criteria, we should seek the advice only from those. whose works we admire or are demonstrated to be superior or admirable in any particular area.

What we should not do is seek advice from or emulate those whose actions have demonstrated the ability to foster disharmony within their circles or conflicts with our values. Recognize that, as we stand today, we have choices that can affect our journey. If we choose to place negative baggage on our wagons, we will be travelling with negative baggage. If however others who have made poor choices attempt to place baggage on your wagon, with self-control you always have the ability to discard any unwanted materials from your wagon. We must consider our wagon as our sanctuary; we take what we choose and cultivate whatever else we need on our journeys.

Passions are to be enjoyed, experiences filled with passions are especially enriching. With self-control we are able to choose if, when, how much and in which passions we partake. With self-control and awareness we are less likely to be manipulated, or even to be predictably reactionary.

When we attain balance, we become more acceptable to others, as they can observe that we are less likely to emotionally unstable or exhibit behaviors that are detrimental to the formation of healthy relationships. Being balanced does not take away from our emotional or physical growth, but there will be an increase in the number of enlightened individuals in the society. These enlightened individuals may in turn reject some of the values and behaviors that are being presented as acceptable in a society by merchants, who because of greed have no care for the well-being of anyone. Even members of their closest circles can be victimized by their actions or the consequences of those actions.

We should all spend some time consciously learning to redirect ourselves. This is a skill that is most beneficial when we encounter tasks which we would rather not perform. Using the breathe, relax, and focus method, we should be able to consciously redirect ourselves to perform those tasks that are needed instead of spending time on activities for which we will need excuses later.

We must also recognize that it is extremely difficult and well nigh impossible for many to transcend the cultures in which they are immersed from birth. Culture can be viewed as a river, if you are born in it, you are wet, and unless you learn to fly, you will always be immersed. Culture is also a foundation and thus we need to be grounded in some culture, so rejection of everything our culture has to offer is also detrimental. We can consciously review and take with us those attributes that are enlightening and serve to brighten our journeys. Recognize that everything we learn is colored by the cultures in which we are immersed and that the truly significant differences between groups are not based in race but are the product of differing cultures.

Spirituality

Just as we can grow physically, we can grow spiritually. Just as our immune system benefits from good food, our spiritual component increases in immunity from detrimental influences, when we perform those exercises that strengthen our spiritual component. Service and sacrifice allows the spiritual component to develop and brings equanimity to our emotional and physical components. Fasting and abstaining from our passions. as well as spending time in meditation, strengthens our spiritual component. Much of our discipline, knowledge and ultimate achievements will come from the development of our spiritual component through the sincere practice of the exercises detailed in this book and others that have been passed down through time. Our spiritual growth is only limited to the degree we allow ourselves to be stunted by the works of others. It is the one area where we can develop a personal sense of belonging and our own conduit to the ultimate Truth, which can become our shield from anything untoward and be a gateway to our transference to a more enlightened being.

Your will is divine, and even when compliance is necessary, never surrender your will to anyone or anything but the Almighty.

GLOSSARY

Village View Principle:

This principle relates to any individuals who would give us advice on how we should conduct ourselves or our personal affairs.

Let's assume for a moment that we all live in a village. We hear a commotion because someone has decided to inform us about something that is about to happen or how we should react to something that is happening.

Well, a crowd gathers and everyone is atwitter about what this person is saying, some agree with them and some don't. Eventually the discussion will inevitably come around to "who is this person?" In the village, this question does not elicit a response only regarding the name of the individual, no, in the village the proper answer to such a question must involve some history of this individual.

We would find out about where they live, how they were raised, what accomplishments they have achieved, who are the members of their family and lot more.

For the purpose of this principle, we must be concerned with anyone willing to give advice or aspires to be in a position where there actions dictate what are acceptable behaviors. We must take a good look at their history to ensure that we are not enabling a hypocrite. Experience should not be purely used to disqualify individuals, just as long as there is coherence and consistency to their actions. Experience and accountability are the key values in accepting the advice of a village speaker, so even past negative episodes in the lives of the speaker do not disqualify them as long as they are can provide valid, credible explanations for these incidents.

We must be especially vigilant of those who try to impose or enforce moral values or standards, especially if they are unwilling or unable to demonstrate consistency in their words and actions. A similar testing should be extended to all those who would seek to be our mentors. Questions to ask for example: Did they raise their own children as they recommend? Have they demonstrated fiscal austerity in their own financial affairs? Do they have relationships that we admire?

This is especially important when we have so many "experts" who seek to influence our behaviors using research and statistics, which can be manipulated for almost any purpose. Regardless of whether the subject is morals, diets, travel, vacations, children, financial matters or relationships, we will all be better served by applying this principle to all those who seek to be our advisers, regardless of whether we requested their advice or not!

Shoplifting principle:

This principle relates to upholding our values regardless of the actions of those with whom we associate, less we pick up unnecessary baggage and incorporate many qualities we despise into our characters.

Imagine this, we are at the store with some friends, because we do not have the money to purchase some items that we would like to have, someone suggests that we steal these items. This creates a significant level of stress and discomfort for us and predictably we are nervous about performing this action, however, in spite of our internal conflicts based on everything we have been taught by those we admire as well as the societal norms, we complete this objectionable action.

Regardless of our need this action may invoke some stress for quite some time. However, that one action may embolden us to become repeat offenders at any point in the future, and we may in time become more comfortable with this despicable behavior to the extent that we may perform it on a regular basis, even when we have the money to make the purchase.

It is the same with lying, cheating or any other morally reprehensible action. Much of the pain of relationships is brought about by those who have succumbed to the "shoplifting" principle, it would be wise therefore that we seek to ensure that, if we have succumbed to participating in this type of behavior, we consciously use our self-control and willpower to repudiate these practices.

Sometimes there are learned behaviors that conflict with both our internal and societal values, nevertheless individuals may incorporate these behaviors during times of stress.

Tow truck driver principle:

This principle relates to among other issues, routine carelessness, lack of preparations or improper personal relations and should not be used as an excuse for not assisting the unfortunate or disenfranchised.

A friend or acquaintance that you care about is about to set out on a journey with which you are familiar. You have travelled this road and know that there are some unpleasant surprises or even serious hazards to be encountered. These can be anything from bumps, potholes, blind turns and even washed out bridges on that road, so the consequences for improper preparations or insufficient care has the potential to be significant. Because of your sense of caring or being aware of certain tendencies in this individual, you decide to offer some advice However, Instead of using to 'village view' principle to determine if your advice is something to be considered, your friend takes this view: "Whoa! Not so fast here now! This is my car, this is my journey! You don't put gas in this car, you don't make payments on this car. Please! I'll drive my car any which way I want, thank you very much!" Not that you didn't expect this reaction if you knew anything about this individual, but you did your part out of a noble and genuine sense of caring.

Some time later you either get a call for help or you encounter that individual stranded at one of the hazards of which you tried to advise, but they chose to ignore. You try to remind them that this could have been avoided, but you are met with "Now, how does that help me now? Right now I need some help to get back on my journey. Would you please not kick me now that I'm down! Are you going to help me or not?".

You decide to 'bite your tongue', roll up your sleeves, get down in the mud and give all the assistance that you can, to fix that tire, get some gas or even to get that car back on it's wheels and back on the road! You may not be ecstatic, but, this is life and the shoe could have been on the other foot. You or someone you care about could be the one stranded, and you sure would appreciate anyone who would stop and help, so you are doing your part... Once the situation has returned to what can be considered normal and this person is once again about to take off on the rest of their journey, you try again to advise of other hazards that you know lie ahead. Not unpredictably you get a "Hey, thanks for stopping and helping, I really appreciate it but..." depending on the individual you get a verbal or non-verbal: "Whoa! Not so fast here now! This is my car, this is my journey! You don't put gas in this car, you don't make payments on this car. Please! I'll drive my car any which way I want, thank you very much!".

While it is noble and spiritually rewarding to help as much as we can, each of us must decide whether we are willing to turn into personal tow truck drivers for individuals who refuse to take responsibility for, or actions to prevent misfortunes. Our help should be unconditional, but we should recognize when those repeated cries for help by the same individuals may be masking their need for growth. The point here is: give assistance as much as, and to as many as you can however, be aware of when your assistance may actually be having a detrimental effect because it enables those who would rely solely on assistance instead of developing their potential to help themselves and eventually growing to be strong enough to be of assistance to others. We are all best served if our help benefit others who in time grow strong and help others, who in time grow strong and...

ABOUT THE AUTHOR

My journey along the path to writing this book started when I was about thirteen or fourteen (don't remember exactly), I had gone fishing by myself one day when I had what is now considered a near death experience, actually, I believe that I died. What I recall from that experience was that I found it difficult to breathe after taking several puffs on a cigarette (yep, I had sneaked away with a couple!). I recall that I simply was unable to get any air into myself and to this day I believe I know what it is like to die, unable to catch my breath, I collapsed into the brush at the side of the lake where I was fishing, what happened next I believe initiated the actions that resulted in this work and the path I have chosen.

For me there were no special lights, no tunnel, none of the 'classical' symptoms associated with near death experiences, I did not even see anyone, but I knew I was not alone. What I felt was that I was in a different place, it felt like a normal day. The one thing that was really different and strange was that I felt this warmth and comfort and I knew instinctively was love. This love however was so strong, so deep, so intense that it felt like a warm wind on my skin and it was as if I was totally enveloped in it. It was then that I heard as if there was a discussion by persons unseen, and a voice or voices then spoke to me saying that I could not stay there and that I "had to go back as no on knew where you are and, your work isn't done yet".

I recall distinctly picking myself up from the ground and dusting the leaves and sand off myself, while feeling groggy and slightly disoriented, however what was most distressing for the following months (while I felt a deep loss at not being in that place) was the feeling of wanting to be back in that place where I could literally feel such deep love. Unbeknownst to my parents or even my closest friends

I even contemplated several ways to get back to that place but I was prevented by the words to which I then had no meaning – I "had to go back because no one knew where you are and your work isn't done yet". I have since learnt that I must treasure this life; this gift from my Creator!

At that time, I sought the company of those who spent a lot of time in churches and seemed to be enlightened. I quickly became disenchanted however, not by their actions (which I accepted as part of life) but by the hypocrisy they exhibited in their day to day lives in the disparity between their words and actions. Eventually I drifted off to just have fun and it's been many years of, well I guess, just drifting.

All these years however I noticed that unlike many around me, I have never felt alone, I always felt that there were those who I could feel even though I could not see who were there to comfort and guide (really in most cases; to rescue!) me. Nonetheless I have never felt alone or lost, and with my memory of my visit to that place when I was a kid, though I was bothered by pain and I treasure His gift, I have never been fearful of the transition we call death.

Although I have always been drawn to churches, I have always been repelled by the hypocrisy and pretentiousness of too many (most?) of the people that I encounter there – so it was at my home that I felt the peace needed to try to get closer to God. It was there that I asked to be given the strength to be a good servant, and begged for the honor of being a part of His plan with no regard for mine or of any man's plan. It was there that I felt the presence of his emissaries and they have communicated with me, they have called my name and woken me repeatedly, with instructions of what to write, it is they who assured me that there are those who wait for these messages, and in time others will accept. They also informed me that there are many who have guided and protected me who will rejoice when this work is done (I have never wondered about distribution of this work, because I know better).

I am a man who has lived a rich and unpretentious life. The path I have walked has allowed me to have such a variety of experiences that I can relate to almost anyone. This in itself is a blessing. I feel fully rewarded just to be able to serve the One who is greater than any other ruler that has, or ever will come into being. I feel a duty to share these three messages and the insight I have gained from His emissaries.